# Lyric Quotation in Plato

# Greek Studies: Interdisciplinary Approaches
Series Editor: Gregory Nagy, Harvard University
Assistant Editor: Timothy Power, Harvard University

**On the front cover**: A calendar frieze representing the Athenian months, reused in the Byzantine Church of the Little Metropolis in Athens. The cross is superimposed, obliterating Taurus of the Zodiac. The choice of this frieze for books in *Greek Studies: Interdisciplinary Approaches* reflects this series' emphasis on the blending of the diverse heritages—Near Eastern, Classical, and Christian—in the Greek tradition. Drawing by Laurie Kain Hart, based on a photograph. Recent titles in the series are:

*Belted Heroes and Bound Women: The Myth of the Homeric Warrior King*
    by Michael J. Bennett, Eckerd College
*Greek Modernism and Beyond*
    edited by Dimitris Tziovas, University of Birmingham
*Aegean Strategies: Studies of Culture and Environment on the European Fringe*
    by P. Nick Kardulias, College of Wooster, and Mark T. Shutes, Youngstown State University
*Aglaia: The Poetry of Alcman, Sappho, Pindar, Bacchylides, and Corinna*
    by Charles Segal, Harvard University
*Eurykleia and Her Successors: Female Figures of Authority in Greek Poetics,*
    by Helen Pournara Karydas, Boston Latin School and Harvard University
*Immortal Armor: The Concept of Alke in Archaic Greek* Poetry
    by Derek Collins, University of Texas at Austin
*Homeric Stitchings: The Homeric Centos of the Empress Eudocia*
    by M. D. Usher, Willamette University
*Recapturing Sophocles' Antigone*
    by William Blake Tyrrell, Michigan State University, and Larry J. Bennett
*Nothing Is As It Seems: The Tragedy of the Implicit in Euripides'* Hippolytus
    by Hanna M. Roisman, Colby College
*Lyric Quotation in Plato*
    by Marian Demos, Florida International University

# Lyric Quotation in Plato

Marian Demos

ROWMAN & LITTLEFIELD PUBLISHERS, INC.
*Lanham • Boulder • New York • Oxford*

ROWMAN & LITTLEFIELD PUBLISHERS, INC.

Published in the United States of America
by Rowman & Littlefield Publishers, Inc.
4720 Boston Way, Lanham, Maryland 20706

12 Hid's Copse Road
Cumnor Hill, Oxford OX2 9JJ, England

Copyright © 1999 by Rowman & Littlefield Publishers, Inc.

*All rights reserved.* No part of this publication may be reproduced, stored in a retrieval system, or transmitted in any form or by any means, electronic, mechanical, photocopying, recording, or otherwise, without the prior permission of the publisher.

British Library Cataloguing in Publication Information Available

**Library of Congress Cataloging-in-Publication Data**

Demos, Marian, 1964-
    Lyric quotation in Plato / Marian Demos.
       p. cm. – (Greek studies)
    Includes bibliographical references and index
    ISBN 978-0-8476-8909-5
    1. Plato—Criticism, Textual. 2. Greek literature—Criticism, Textual. 3. Quotations, Greek. I. Title. II. Series.
PA4291.D46 1999
184—dc21                                                      98-36861
                                                                                   CIP

Printed in the United States of America

♾™ The paper used in this publication meets the minimum requirements of American National Standard for Information Sciences—Permanence of Paper for Printed Library Materials, ANSI Z39.48–1984.

## Contents

| | |
|---|---:|
| Foreword | vii |
| Acknowledgments | ix |
| 1. Introduction | 1 |
| 2. Simonides' Ode to Scopas in the *Protagoras* | 11 |
| 3. Callicles' Quotation of Pindar in the *Gorgias* | 39 |
| 4. Stesichorus' Palinode in the *Phaedrus* | 65 |
| 5. Conclusion | 87 |
| Bibliography | 89 |
| Index | 97 |
| About the Author | 101 |

GREEK STUDIES:
INTERDISCIPLINARY APPROACHES

# FOREWORD

GREGORY NAGY, GENERAL EDITOR

Building on the foundations of scholarship within the disciplines of philology, philosophy, history, and archeology, this series spans the continuum of Greek traditions extending from the second millennium B.C.E. to the present, not just the Archaic and Classical periods. The aim is to enhance perspectives by applying various disciplines to problems that have in the past been treated as the exclusive concern of a single given discipline. Besides the crossing-over of the other disciplines, as in the case of historical and literary studies, the series encourages the application of such newer ones as linguistics, sociology, anthropology, and comparative literature. It also encourages encounters with current trends in methodology, especially in the realm of literary theory.

*Lyric Quotation in Plato*, by Marian Demos, is a study of Plato's command of Greek literary traditions, with specific reference to lyric poetry in its performative as well as compositional dimensions. As test cases, Demos has selected three celebrated lyric "quotations" within the respective contexts of three celebrated Platonic works: the *Protagoras*, the *Gorgias*, and the *Phaedrus*.

The first chapter introduces us to the study. The second centers on the problem of interpreting correctly a lyric poem by Simonides as "quoted" in the *Protagoras*. It is argued that Plato has Socrates provide a fundamentally sound approach to understanding the intended meaning of Simonides' words. By contrast, Protagoras is portrayed as having introduced the discussion of the poem's meaning in such a way as to fit in his own sophistic agenda, that is, to make the lyric poet Simonides most vulnerable to the charge of self-contradiction. The third chapter contends that Plato has Callicles "misquote" Pindar in the *Gorgias* in order to animate the character of Callicles—and to suit the immediate context of the Pindaric reference. The fourth chapter highlights Socrates' "quotation," in the *Phaedrus*, of Stesichorus' notorious song of recantation, the Palinode to Helen. Like Stesichorus, Socrates composes an ad hoc palinode. This time, the recantation is not a song about Helen but a speech about Eros. Like the lyric poet, the philosopher seeks to avert potential divine retribution.

Socrates' comments to the young Phaedrus regarding love and poetry as types of divine inspiration reflect his own poetic "inspiration" in the dialogue. By extension, Plato reflects his own poetic education through his skill in making famous lyric songs come back to life. Such is the power of lyric "quotation."

# ACKNOWLEDGMENTS

I wish to express my gratitude to Gregory Nagy, the editor of this series, for his encouragement and for sharing with me his many insights on the role of lyric poetry during Plato's time. I would also like to acknowledge my debt to Charles Segal and Ian Rutherford, each of whom offered me valuable comments and suggestions on a wide variety of topics. Albert Henrichs also greatly influenced my understanding of Plato's style.

The editors of *Harvard Studies in Classical Philology* and *Classical World* kindly granted permission to reprint chapters three and four respectively, which previously appeared in their publications. Excerpts from R. Hackforth's translation of the *Phaedrus* are reprinted with the permission of Cambridge University Press; excerpts from W. K. C. Guthrie's translation of the *Protagoras* are reprinted with the kind permission of Penguin Books, Ltd.

I would like to thank Karen Johnson and Robin Adler of Rowman & Littlefield for their guidance, and Maura Giles for her assistance in preparing my manuscript for publication. The Center for Hellenic Studies made it possible for me to finish this book during my stay there as a Summer Fellow in 1997. I am also grateful to the American Association of University Women for its financial support. Finally, I wish to acknowledge the very generous support I have received from Florida International University.

# 1

## INTRODUCTION

The subject of this study is Plato's incorporation of lyric poetry into the fabric of his own work. Although much has been written about Plato's views on poetry, as revealed explicitly in the *Republic* and the *Laws*, few studies have been concerned with Plato's own use of poetry.[1] The dialogues are replete with poetic allusion, by paraphrase and by quotation. This could be perceived as paradoxical in light of Plato's proposal to banish poets from his ideal *polis*.[2] However, if we take into account the tradition of literary criticism embedded in Greek literature from Homer forward,[3] Plato's relationship with poetic works that were already considered classics by his own time seems far less anomalous.

Any discussion of Greek views on poetry necessitates the understanding that for the Greeks the essence of poetry lies in its capacity to delight and to instruct. In the words of E. E. Sikes, "the history of Greek criticism is largely occupied, not so much with a denial of the function of art to teach, as with the relation between this teaching and the claim of pleasure to be its immediate end."[4] Although this observation may be generally valid,

---

1. Moravcsik and Temko (eds.) 1982 provide a sampling of the varied approaches to the general topic of Plato's philosophical views on the nature of poetry as a mimetic art.

2. Cf. *Republic* 3.398a, 10.595a ff., 607a and *Laws* 7.817c (with respect to the banishment of tragic poets).

3. Cf. Sikes 1931 for a survey of the tradition of Greek "literary criticism"; Maehler 1963 discusses the self-stylized role of the archaic Greek poet. Lanata 1963 provides important texts with Italian translation and commentary.

4. Sikes 1931.1.

Sikes does not explain the type of instruction poetry is meant to provide.[5] Aristophanes, for example, has Aeschylus say in the *Frogs* (ll. 1054-55) that poets are responsible for the teaching of adults. Poetry, as a medium for recording the glorious deeds of men (κλέα ἀνδρῶν),[6] is itself the bestower of glory upon the deeds of gods and men.[7]

Note that Odysseus says that either the Muse or Apollo taught (viii 488: ἐδίδαξε) the bard Demodocus to sing and that Hesiod himself claims that the Muses taught him lovely song (*Th.* 22: καλὴν ἐδίδαξαν ἀοιδήν). The poet therefore is a teacher insofar as his own instruction by the Muses is transmitted to the audience by way of his song. It can then be said that the power of a poet, who is taught and inspired by the Muses, is his ability to choose his subject and treat it in whatever way he sees fit. Such a view is intimated by Hesiod in the *Theogony* when he describes what the Muses said when they inspired (l. 31: ἐνέπνευσαν) him with a divine voice:

ἴδμεν ψεύδεα πολλὰ λέγειν ἐτύμοισιν ὁμοῖα,
ἴδμεν δ', εὖτ' ἐθέλωμεν, ἀληθέα γηρύσασθαι.
(*Th.* 27-28)

We know to tell many falsehoods that resemble truth,
but we know to sing true things when we wish.

We may infer that Hesiod, like the Muses, is capable of speaking not only true things but also many false things that resemble truth. This is a divine sort of power that mortals may obtain only through inspiration.

Pindar takes the metaphor of divine inspiration to even greater lengths, as he envisions himself as a prophet of the Muse. He invites the Muse to prophesy and declares that he will be her prophet: μαντεύεο, Μοῖσα, προφατεύσω δ' ἐγώ (fr. 150

---

5. Russell 1981 (chapter 6) discusses "the poet as teacher."
6. *Odyssey* viii 73.
7. Cf. Nagy 1979 *passim* for a discussion of the power of poetry to confer glory (κλέος).

Snell-Maehler).⁸ The source of knowledge (σοφία) for both the poet and the seer is the same: divine inspiration. The notion that poets have special relationships with Muses is a familiar one; however, Pindar makes it clear that inspiration is related to the poet's being σοφός by nature: σοφὸς ὁ πολλὰ εἰδὼς φυᾷ (*Ol.* 2.86). The divinely inspired knowledge of an encomiastic poet like Pindar lends authority to his conferral of praise or blame. Consequently, Pindar can criticize even Homer, his predecessor in the poetic tradition, on the grounds that Homer's poetic skill (σοφία) misleads men into attributing more fame to Odysseus than he deserved (cf. *Nem.* 7.20-27). Such a comment regarding a poet's power to deceive his audience by the charm of his words is striking in the context of a poem; Pindar is obliquely self-referential. He appropriates for himself the power that he ascribes to Homer. While Pindar criticizes Homer for bestowing excessive praise, he disapproves of Archilochus' excessive fondness for blaming (*Pyth.* 2.52-56). Pindar views Archilochus as an unwitting victim of his own predilection for speaking ill (κακαγορία), and describes his predecessor as fond of blaming (ψογερός). It is interesting to note that Pindar, within the context of an epinician ode, is blaming a past poet for misusing blame (ψόγος) poetry.

Since any poet, epic or lyric, can confer praise or blame, it can be said that his work is moralistic by its very nature. Passing judgment is a deontological activity that condemns or recommends behavior that is consistent with an established ethical code. By glorifying the deeds—both praiseworthy and objectionable—of gods and men, the poet becomes a transmitter of moral values and, as such, an obvious target of attack. Xenophanes, the sixth-century Ionian philosophical poet who composed in a variety of meters, is the first to attack Homer and Hesiod for their portrayal of the gods. The criticism, like the poetry it attacks, is composed in hexameters:

---

8. For a discussion of the relationship between prophet (προφήτης) and seer (μάντις), see Nagy 1990.163 regarding the interchangeability of these terms and the notion that "the prophecy of the *mantis* and the poetry formulated by the *prophetes* are...one."

πάντα θεοῖς ἀνέθηκαν ″Ομηρός θ' Ἡσίοδός τε
ὅσσα παρ' ἀνθρώποισιν ὀνείδεα καὶ ψόγος ἐστίν,
κλέπτειν μοιχεύειν τε καὶ ἀλλήλους ἀπατεύειν.
(Diels-Kranz 21 B 11)

Homer and Hesiod attributed to the gods all
things that are shameful and blameworthy among men,
theft, adultery and deceiving one another.

Xenophanes is generally thought to be "the first person on record to condemn the epic explicitly on moral grounds."[9] In response to this sort of criticism, which focuses on the immorality of myths found in poetry, allegorical interpretations of traditional poetry are offered by such figures as Theagenes of Rhegium in the sixth century and Anaxagoras in the fifth. Allegorical interpretations of poems defend the value of poetry as a didactic medium from which one can learn about the physical universe as well as about moral questions.

By the fourth century, poetry is no longer the only medium to form the basis for a person's education. Rhetoric and philosophy infiltrate the domain of παιδεία that poetry, both epic and lyric, had claimed for its own. More importantly, poetry becomes the object of study for both sophists and philosophers alike. Gorgias, for example, in his *Encomium of Helen* discusses poetry at length, especially its power to influence human emotions;[10] like prose, poetry is viewed as a powerful tool that can be manipulated for a pragmatic purpose.[11] Other sophists, notably Protagoras and Prodicus, study poetical works with a philological bent. Plato often refers to their preoccupation with correct wording (ὀρθοέπεια).[12] I will say more regarding the sophists in my chapter on the exegesis of Simonidean poetry in the *Protagoras*.

The sophists are not alone in their scrutiny of the technical and stylistic aspects of poetry. Aristophanes, recognizing the impact of dramatic poetry, especially tragedy, on the *polis*, not

---

9. Russell 1981.87.
10. Cf. Gorgias, *Helen* 8f.
11. Cf. Sikes 1931.27-36; Russell 1981.22-24.
12. See, for example, the *Protagoras* and the *Cratylus*.

only parodies the poetic language of the tragedians but also makes literary criticism the subject of his comedy the *Frogs*. Euripides, asked by Aeschylus about the qualities that characterize a good poet, remarks that a poet's—more precisely, his own—technical skill and counsel with a view toward making men in the cities better are worthy of admiration: δεξιότητος καὶ νουθεσίας, ὅτι βελτίους τε ποιοῦμεν τοὺς ἀνθρώπους ἐν ταῖς πόλεσιν (*Frogs* 1009). Aristophanes places this comment in the mouth of the upstart Euripides for comic effect, since the *agôn* of the play pits the old-fashioned Aeschylus against the irreverent Euripides. Specifically, Aristophanes condemns the new tragic poetry of Euripides and advocates a reversion to the older sort of tragedy as composed by Aeschylus.

Morality, as transmitted through the theater, is a central issue for Aristophanes. We need only recall the words of Pluto in the *exodos* (ll. 1501-1503), which indicate that the primary function of the tragic poet is as teacher: 'save our city by your good advice and instruct the foolish' (σῷζε πόλιν τὴν ἡμετέραν γνώμαις ἀγαθαῖς, καὶ παίδευσον τοὺς ἀνοήτους). The fact that in the *Frogs* Aristophanes criticizes contemporary dramatic poetry—as exemplified by Euripides—on stylistic and moral grounds highlights the prominence of dramatic poetry, as compared to epic and lyric, within the Athenian social context by the end of the fifth century.[13] The nostalgic longing for the older poetry of the tragedian Aeschylus that characterizes the *Frogs* resembles the "back to basics" approach to education advocated by the character Strepsiades in the *Clouds*. Strepsiades says that his confrontation with his son Pheidippides, an admirer of Euripides' poetry, began when his son refused to take up the lyre and sing a Simonidean song after dinner:

καὶ μὴν ὅθεν γε πρῶτον ἠρξάμεσθα λοιδορεῖσθαι
ἐγὼ φράσω. 'πειδὴ γὰρ εἰστιώμεθ', ὥσπερ ἴστε,
πρῶτον μὲν αὐτὸν τὴν λύραν λαβόντ' ἐγὼ 'κέλευσα
ᾆσαι Σιμωνίδου μέλος, τὸν Κριόν, ὡς ἐπέχθη.

---

13. Cf. Nagy 1989.66-69; he calls attention to Old Comedy's "dramatised alienation from everything that happens to be current" and "the evolving predominance of Athenian theatre as the primary poetic medium" (p. 66).

ὁ δ' εὐθέως ἀρχαῖον εἶν' ἔφασκε τὸ κιθαρίζειν
ᾄδειν τε πίνονθ', ὡσπερεὶ κάχρυς γυναῖκ' ἀλοῦσαν.
(*Clouds* 1353-1358)

I will tell you when we first began to reproach each other. When we were feasting, as you know, I first asked him to take up the lyre and sing a song of Simonides, "How the ram was shorn." But he immediately said that it was old-fashioned to play the cithara and to sing while drinking, and he compared this to a woman grinding wheat.

Pheidippides, we are told, regards performing lyrical compositions after dinner as passé. He even dares to call Simonides a bad poet: καὶ τὸν Σιμωνίδην ἔφασκ' εἶναι κακὸν ποιητήν (1362). Strepsiades then asks his son to recite, without musical accompaniment, some lines of Aeschylus; Pheidippides proceeds to criticize the old-fashioned tragic poet Aeschylus, who is regarded by his father as foremost among poets (1366: πρῶτον ἐν ποιηταῖς). The performance of lyrical compositions by educated symposiasts is of course obsolete by Aristophanes' time; however, Strepsiades is portrayed as nostalgic for the good old days when a sound education in the classics presupposed the ability not only to recite but also to sing lyric works and accompany oneself on a musical instrument like the cithara.[14] Strepsiades' preference for the older, more august tragedies of Aeschylus instead of the newer works of Euripides is similar to the verdict of Dionysus in the *Frogs*; in both plays, Aeschylus, as opposed to Euripides, is represented as part of the established poetic heritage of the *polis*. Aristophanes' plays, therefore, are works of literary criticism, since they not only parody the particular themes and types of diction found in the works of

---

14. Cf. Protagoras' comments on the musical education of wealthy young men such as Pericles' sons in the latter half of the fifth century (*Prot.* 325e-326c). After having read and memorized poetry while at school in order to learn about and emulate the noble figures of the past, youths are taught to play the lyre and to perform the works of the lyric poets (326a7-b1: ἐπειδὰν κιθαρίζειν μάθωσιν, ἄλλων αὖ ποιητῶν ἀγαθῶν ποιήματα διδάσκουσι μελοποιῶν, εἰς τὰ κιθαρίσματα ἐντείνοντες...). See also the comments of the anonymous Athenian interlocutor in *Laws* 810e6-813a3.

Aeschylus and Euripides but also highlight the central role of poetry and music in the sphere of civic education.

Like Aristophanes, Plato is a literary critic insofar as he is concerned with the impact of poetry and music (μουσική) upon education. He too is concerned with the moral instruction poetry is assumed to provide. Aristophanes, however, is himself a poet; he accepts poetry's exalted status in society as a given, and it is through the poetic medium that Aristophanes calls attention to the use—and potential abuse—of that medium. Plato, on the other hand, regards philosophy as the supreme educational medium that ought to exert the greatest influence upon a man's mind and character.[15] In other words, dialectic, as exemplified by its greatest practitioner, Socrates, is superior to poetry because its essence is not irrational and it serves as a better guide in the search for truth. Although a detailed discussion of Plato's complex views on poetry in general is beyond the scope of this study, it is important that we focus on Plato's inheritance of the poetic tradition fundamental to education in Greek society.[16] Even if Plato criticizes poetry on moral and epistemological grounds, his work presupposes a thorough familiarity with the poetic tradition that he proposes to uproot. We may surmise that Plato would agree with the observation that it is justifiable to dismiss a body of knowledge as unworthy of study only after one's mastery of it has led to the questioning of its authority. My subsequent analysis of Plato's quotations from the lyric poets is based upon this paradox. This study concentrates on three lyric quotations: the Simonides poem in the *Protagoras*, Callicles' reference to Pindar in the *Gorgias*, and Socrates' use of Stesichorus' "palinode" in the *Phaedrus*.[17]

In Books II and III of the *Republic*, Plato has Socrates reject poetry on moral grounds. The stories related by the poets,

---

15. Note Socrates' own mention of the 'ancient disagreement between philosophy and poetry' (*Rep.* 607b5-6: παλαιὰ μέν τις διαφορὰ φιλοσοφίᾳ τε καὶ ποιητικῇ).

16. Socrates himself refers to the love of poetry nurtured by city-states in *Rep.* 607e7-8.

17. See Vicaire 1960.129-149 for other examples of lyric quotation in Plato's dialogues. Tarrant 1951.59-67 discusses Plato's use of quotations from poets, especially from Homer, and argues that they form the bulk of his "illustrative material."

especially Homer and Hesiod, concerning the behavior of the gods are considered immoral and therefore are not suitable for the education of the "guardians" of the ideal *polis* (377b-378e). Even the poetry of the tragic theater is not spared from criticism. Plato has Socrates quote a passage from the *Niobe* of Aeschylus (fr. 162 Nauck) as an example of impious and false utterance regarding gods and heroes (391e7-11). Worst of all, the words of the poets can be harmful to the souls of those who hear them: καὶ μὴν τοῖς γε ἀκούουσιν βλαβερά (391e4).[18] Socrates continues in Book III with his prescriptions concerning the other components of song (398d1: τὸ μέλος), namely, 'the organization of pitches' (ἁρμονία)[19] and 'rhythm' (ῥυθμός). He concludes that having a "good" disposition or character is a precondition for one's displaying all the elements of "good" song: εὐλογία ἄρα καὶ εὐαρμοστία καὶ εὐσχημοσύνη καὶ εὐρυθμία εὐηθείᾳ ἀκολουθεῖ (400d11-e1).

Plato's criticism of poetry as a "mimetic" art is too complex a topic for a brief investigation into his treatment of the lyric poets. Nevertheless, the following observations must be made. First, Plato in Book X of the *Republic* has Socrates consider most poetry (with the exception of hymns to the gods and eulogies of praiseworthy men) a mimetic art that has no place in his ideal city-state.[20] It is argued that poets, like painters, create imitations of reality that are inferior to reality and appeal to the irrational or inferior part of the soul (605a-c). Second, poets have the power to corrupt the "city-state" of the soul by placing a spell over the listener. In the presence of poetry's power to bewitch the listener,[21] Socrates urges the chanting of a

---

18. As Russell 1981.90 succinctly remarks: "Indeed, the better the poetry, the worse the moral effect."

19. Cf. Barker 1984.130 for this translation of ἁρμονία and for a detailed study of this passage concerning music (397a-401b). Plato returns to the topic of musical education in *Laws* 654a-672e.

20. See 607a3-5 for the reference to hymns and encomia as the two "permissible" genres; cf. *Laws* 801e1-802b1. Perhaps Plato allows for them because he believes they instill a pious attitude toward divine and heroic figures; i.e., poetry is "good" only when it "imitates" the ideal form of "the good" by calling attention to "particular" examples of goodness (e.g., virtuous deeds associated with heroes).

21. Socrates emphasizes the spellbinding effect of poetry at 607c7.

'counterspell' (608a4: ἐπῳδή) that prevents one from taking poetry seriously (608a6-b2). Plato has Socrates refer specifically to lyric (or "melic") poetry as one type of mimetic poetry that ought to be banned (607a5; cf. 607d4).

The views Plato expresses regarding poetry in his last work, the *Laws*, resemble those of the *Republic*. However, now the poets are not expelled outright; rather, they are to be heavily censored. The ideal lawgiver would insist that poets employ diction and music representative of, and conducive to, correct behavior (660a3-8; cf. 801c8-d6). A specialized knowledge of poetry and its concomitant musical element is here considered essential to a "liberal education." The poet himself must be a virtuous man in order to compose good poetry. In the words of D. A. Russell, "the acceptable poet of the *Laws* is a good man in his way: over fifty years of age, having served the state with credit, he is now allowed under licence to compose poems of praise and blame."[22] The traditional Greek concept of the poet's role as educator of the *polis* is reaffirmed in the *Laws*.

Although Plato makes a conscious effort to dissociate himself from the tradition that makes poetry the chief educational medium, the dialogues themselves indicate that he is greatly influenced by poetry, especially epic and lyric. Socratic diction is filled with casual references to the words of the poets, thereby displaying Plato's own knowledge of poetry. Often, however, the quotations play a vital role in their respective contexts. The quotation of Simonides in the *Protagoras*, for example, provides an opportunity for exegesis on the part of Socrates and his interlocutor while simultaneously allowing Plato to promote his own vision of the optimal method of discourse among educated men. As I will argue, Callicles' quotation of Pindar in the *Gorgias* subtly reveals much concerning the character of one of Socrates' most eloquent opponents. In addition, Socrates' "palinode," as compared to Stesichorus' recanting of his earlier defamation of Helen, serves as a framework for his own poetic and ritualistic language in the *Phaedrus*. An appreciation of the significance of these references to lyric poetry within their respective contexts is the ultimate goal of this study.

---

22. Russell 1981.104.

2

## SIMONIDES' ODE TO SCOPAS
## IN THE *PROTAGORAS*

One of the most controversial topics in the study of Greek lyric poetry centers on Simonides' poem to Scopas and its role in the *Protagoras*. Uncertainties remain concerning the genre to which the poem belongs, the poem's original setting and intent, and the interpretations of the poem by Protagoras and Socrates. Scholars have attempted to reconstruct Simonides' poem from the quotations in the Platonic dialogue and thus have isolated it from the only context in which it has come down to us.[1] My purpose in studying Simonides' poem and its interpretation in the *Protagoras* is not to argue for any definitive text of the poem and thereby divorce it from the context of the dialogue.

My interest lies in Socrates' interpretation of the poem and the poem's role in the conversation between Socrates and Protagoras. I believe that Socrates' represented interpretation is fundamentally sound and that this section of the dialogue, which some consider a comic digression on Plato's part, has a serious intent. Plato has Socrates view the meaning of Simonides' words from a "Socratic" standpoint. As we shall see, Socrates ascribes his own philosophical tenets to Simonides. If Socrates' statements regarding Simonides' poem seem ludicrous to us, perhaps we are lacking the knowledge that Plato's—not to mention Socrates'—intended audience possessed regarding the poem under discussion. It is important to notice at the very

---

1. Gentili 1964.274 ff. offers a full bibliography on Simonides' poem. For more recent treatments, see Parry 1965.297-320, Donlan 1969.71-95, Dickie 1978.21-33, Most 1989.103, and Carson 1992.110-130. Recent philosophical (rather than philological) studies include Goldberg 1983.156-220, Frede 1986.729-753, and Scodel 1986.25-27.

beginning of any study of Simonides' poem that the poem is not quoted in its entirety. Extrapolation on the part of scholars therefore becomes necessary but, in some cases, may lead to conclusions that appear as unfathomable as Socrates' own interpretation.

Protagoras is coerced into asking questions of Socrates so that the discussion regarding ἀρετή ('virtue') can continue (339a-d). However, the inquiry is now transferred to the realm of poetry (339a5-6: τὸ ἐρώτημα...μετενηνεγμένον δ' εἰς ποίησιν), and the role of poetry in a man's παιδεία ('education') has become the focus of the discussion (338e7). The significance of the episode in the *Protagoras* involving the interpretation of verses from Simonides' ode to Scopas is difficult to grasp because Plato appears to portray Socrates as unable to provide a convincing defense of the meaning of the verses quoted by Protagoras. The sophist claims that Simonides contradicts himself, since he makes two seemingly contrasting statements in the same poem. First, Protagoras quotes the following lines (presumably the beginning of the poem):[2]

ἄνδρ' ἀγαθὸν μὲν ἀλαθέως γενέσθαι χαλεπόν,
χερσίν τε καὶ ποσὶ καὶ νόῳ τετράγωνον, ἄνευ ψόγου
τετυγμένον.

(339b1-3)

Hard is it on the one hand to become
A good man truly, hands and feet and mind
Foursquare, wrought without blame.[3]

Socrates claims that he knows this poem very well and that it is composed correctly (339b8). Protagoras asks Socrates whether a poem is well-constructed if the poet contradicts himself; Socrates says that it doubtless is not. The sophist proceeds to quote more of Simonides' poem:

---

2. Throughout my discussion, I print Simonides' lines as they appear in the *OCT* edition of the dialogue.

3. The English translation of select passages of the *Protagoras* is that of W. K. C. Guthrie in Hamilton and Cairns (eds.) 1961.308-52, used with permission of Penguin Books, Ltd.

οὐδέ μοι ἐμμελέως τὸ Πιττάκειον νέμεται,
καίτοι σοφοῦ παρὰ φωτὸς εἰρημένον· χαλεπὸν φάτ'
ἐσθλὸν ἔμμεναι.

(339c3-5)

Nor do I count as sure the oft-quoted word
of Pittacus, though wise indeed he was
Who spoke it. To be noble, said the sage,
Is hard.

Protagoras then asks Socrates if all the lines he quoted belong to one and the same poet and if the latter words are in accordance with the former. According to Socrates, the two quotations agree with one another; however, in an aside, he expresses his apprehension regarding Protagoras' seemingly purposeful line of questioning (339c8-9: καὶ ἅμα μέντοι ἐφοβούμην μὴ τὶ λέγοι—'and yet I feared that he may have a point').

Protagoras' questions make it clear that he intends to criticize Simonides' poetic skill. I take it that when Protagoras says that the poet 'does not speak correctly' (οὐκ ὀρθῶς λέγει), he is referring to a flaw in the logic of a poem's overall meaning or intent.[4] Since Simonides had first stated that it is difficult for a man to be good truly, he seems to be inconsistent when he criticizes a similar remark by Pittacus (339c4-5: χαλεπὸν φάτ' ἐσθλὸν ἔμμεναι—'he said it is difficult to be noble'). Before looking closely at the lines attributed to Simonides, it is important to ask why Socrates feels compelled to uphold Simonides' integrity as a poet. Is Socrates really concerned with Simonides' meaning, or is he intent upon countering Protagoras' display of knowledge with respect to poetry only to present any type of challenge that he can muster against the sophist? The latter is the more probable, since Socrates himself views his confrontation with Protagoras as a sort of bout. The language Socrates uses to describe the effect of Protagoras' "blow" belongs to a boxing

---

4. Protagoras' condemnation of Simonides' logic is explicit in 339d. That Protagoras was fond of criticizing poets is attested by Aristotle (*Poet.* 1456b15) who regards Protagoras' pedantic criticism of the *Iliad's* first line as unfounded.

match: ὡσπερεὶ ὑπὸ ἀγαθοῦ πύκτου πληγείς, ἐσκοτώθην τε καὶ ἰλιγγίασα ( 339e1-2: 'things went dark and I felt dizzy, as if I had been hit by a good boxer'.) If one considers the exchange between the two as an *agôn* in which Socrates is intent upon demonstrating that Protagoras is not as keen a literary critic (or one who ranks himself as *sophos* as the poets) as he himself thinks, then the validity of Socrates' argumentation becomes secondary. Socrates confesses that he appeals to Prodicus the Cean in the immediate audience in order to have time to think about what Simonides meant in the poem under discussion (339e3-5). Socrates puts his appeal in the language of Homer, quoting *Iliad* 21.308-9, and views Simonides as though the poet were a citadel in need of protection from the attack of Protagoras.[5]

Earlier in the *Protagoras*, Prodicus is portrayed as a sophist particularly keen on semantic differences;[6] a touch of humor on the part of Plato is obvious in Prodicus' monologue at 337a1-c4 where he goes on at tedious length to distinguish between the meanings of verbs. This was a hallmark of his "sophistry," or, as Socrates politely says in 340a8, his μουσική (poetical sensibility and education), and Plato does not hesitate to exploit the comic possibilities that such a practice can offer. Since Prodicus knows how to distinguish meanings, Socrates begins to discuss whether Simonides' statement that "it is difficult for a man to become (γενέσθαι) good truly" is the same as Pittacus' saying that "it is difficult to be (ἔμμεναι) good" (340c4-5). Since 'to become' is different from 'to be', as Socrates maintains and believes that Prodicus—given his love of semantic distinctions—would doubtless agree, then Socrates concludes that Simonides is not contradicting himself when he disagrees with Pittacus' remark. In order to strengthen his argument, Socrates paraphrases *Works and Days* 289 and 291-2, where Hesiod describes ἀρετή as something difficult to achieve but easy to

---

5. Note Socrates' use of the ethical dative ἡμῖν when he refers to Protagoras' "destruction" of Simonides, a matter involving both Socrates and Prodicus: ἀτὰρ καὶ ἐγὼ σὲ παρακαλῶ, μὴ ἡμῖν ὁ Πρωταγόρας τὸν Σιμωνίδην ἐκπέρσῃ (340a6-7).

6. Cf. *Protagoras* 340a, 340c, 358a, 358d; *Meno* 75e; *Laches* 197b-d; *Charmides* 163b-d; and *Euthydemus* 277e-278a.

possess once one reaches its summit (340d1-5). Socrates probably has in mind another of Simonides' poems, *PMG* 579, which resembles the Hesiodic passage as it contains a reference to virtue dwelling atop steep cliffs; the diction of both Hesiod and Simonides is similar.⁷ Prodicus agrees with Socrates' interpretation of the subtle difference between the words of Simonides and Pittacus; however, Protagoras immediately disagrees with Socrates' argument that Simonides regards virtue as something easy (φαῦλον) to possess on the grounds that all men deem it the most difficult thing of all (πάντων χαλεπώτατον).

Protagoras' question to Socrates about the lines from Simonides is intended to show us more about Protagoras, the sophist who ranks himself among the great poets whom he

---

7. Cf. Hesiod, *Works and Days* 289-292:
    τῆς δ' ἀρετῆς <u>ἱδρῶτα</u> θεοὶ προπάροιθεν ἔθηκαν
    ἀθάνατοι· μακρὸς δὲ καὶ ὄρθιος οἶμος ἐς αὐτὴν
    καὶ τρηχὺς τὸ πρῶτον· ἐπὴν δ' <u>εἰς ἄκρον ἵκηται</u>,
    ῥηιδίη δὴ ἔπειτα πέλει, χαλεπή περ ἐοῦσα

    The immortal gods have placed sweat on the path to virtue;
    the path is long and steep,
    and rough at first. When one reaches the top,
    the road, which before had been difficult, becomes easy

    to the Simonides fragment (*PMG* 579):
    ἐστί τις λόγος
    τὰν Ἀρετὰν ναίειν δυσαμβάτοισ' ἐπὶ πέτραις,
    †νῦν δέ μιν θοαν† χῶραν ἁγνὸν ἀμφέπειν·
    οὐδὲ πάντων βλεφάροισι θνατῶν
    ἔσοπτος, ὧι μὴ δακέθυμος <u>ἱδρὼς</u>
    ἔνδοθεν μόληι,
    <u>ἵκηι τ' ἐς ἄκρον</u> ἀνδρείας.

    There is a story
    that Virtue dwells on rocks which are hard to climb,
    [...] looks after the holy ground.
    She is not visible to the eyes of all mortal men,
    but only to him whose heart-eating sweat comes from within,
    the one who attains the peak of manliness.

views as sophists in disguise. Unlike the poets, Protagoras is not afraid of displaying his knowledge (σοφιστικὴ τέχνη); in other words, Plato is setting Protagoras up as one who considers himself among the great educators of Hellas. Plato has Protagoras characterize Homer, Hesiod, and, interestingly enough, Simonides as sophists:

> ἐγὼ δὲ τὴν σοφιστικὴν τέχνην φημὶ μὲν εἶναι παλαιάν, τοὺς δὲ μεταχειριζομένους αὐτὴν τῶν παλαιῶν ἀνδρῶν, φοβουμένους τὸ ἐπαχθὲς αὐτῆς, πρόσχημα ποιεῖσθαι καὶ προκαλύπτεσθαι, τοὺς μὲν ποίησιν, οἷον Ὅμηρόν τε καὶ Ἡσίοδον καὶ Σιμωνίδην...
>
> (316d3-e5)
>
> Personally I hold that the sophist's art is an ancient one, but that those who put their hand to it in former times, fearing the odium which it brings, adopted a disguise and worked under cover. Some used poetry as a screen, for instance, Homer and Hesiod and Simonides...

These are bold words. Protagoras has the audacity not only to liken himself to such figures but also to claim that he surpasses them because he alone does not deny being a sophist; like these ἄνδρες παλαιοί, he educates men (317b4-5: ὁμολογῶ τε σοφιστὴς εἶναι καὶ παιδεύειν ἀνθρώπους—'I admit that I am a sophist and educator').

Since, in his own eyes, his knowledge is equal if not superior to the poet's, Protagoras can criticize Simonides' poem. Consequently, Socrates' reaction to Protagoras' attack on Simonides can be understood as an attempt to preserve the stature of a traditional transmitter of παιδεία, in the case of Simonides, the poet-educator for the χορός, and to reject the audacious claims of the sophist. Thus, if Protagoras objects to Simonides' poem, greater objections should be raised against the sophist who claims to be such a great educator, especially in the sphere of ἀρετή. Moreover, if Protagoras displays his lack of ἀρετή by posing a question that does not do justice to Simonides' poem as a whole, then it is possible to view Socrates' "literary criticism" with respect to the Simonidean quotations as not simply a misunderstanding of the poem's meaning on the part of Socrates but as a poor answer to a question that was unfair from the beginning, since it took the quotations out of their original context.

It is usually assumed that Protagoras quoted the beginning of Simonides' poem.[8] Perhaps Protagoras omitted lines known to the readers for whom Plato intended the dialogue. The poem in its entirety may have been well-known to the immediate audience. Unfortunately, the entire text of Simonides' poem is not extant. Some of Socrates' comments may not have been as out of place as they now seem. Although this is a possible explanation for the seemingly unintelligible line of argumentation offered by Socrates in his defense of Simonides, one must not exclude the scenario that Socrates cannot offer an adequate justification of the poem's meaning because Protagoras has skewed the question-and-answer session in his favor; that is, the way that Protagoras sets up the charge of self-contradiction against Simonides does not permit any suitable rebuttal.

Socrates again consults Prodicus as an authority on the meanings of words. Before a discussion of what Simonides meant by χαλεπόν ('difficult': 341a5-d7), Plato has Socrates infuse his words to Prodicus, another sophist in the group, with a mocking tone. He is surely ironic in saying that Prodicus' presence during the exchange with Protagoras is fortuitous (340e8-9). This somewhat sarcastic tone continues when he states that Prodicus has some sort of divine knowledge that dates back to the days of Simonides or even earlier. Surely Protagoras would agree, since he himself had compared his own knowledge to that of 'the men of old' earlier in the dialogue (316d and following). Socrates then is attacking indirectly the sophist Protagoras when he describes the sophist Prodicus in these terms. Socrates' saying that he is a student of Prodicus takes this ironical tone to an extreme and, as if he were pitting one sophist against another sophist, he claims that he is more expert than Protagoras in the field of semantic differentiation because he can apply Prodicus' expertise to the matter at hand (341a2-4).

---

8. Socrates' statement at 343c7-9 implies that Protagoras quoted from the very beginning of the poem. However, τὸ πρῶτον τοῦ ᾄσματος need not refer specifically to the poem's first line.

The interpretation of Socrates' appeal to Prodicus as a means of mocking "sophists" in general is supported by the subsequent passage on the meaning of Simonides' use of χαλεπόν. Once Prodicus claims that Simonides meant χαλεπόν in the sense of κακόν ('bad' or 'evil': 341c2), a definition swiftly rejected by Protagoras, and once Socrates agrees with the latter and withdraws Prodicus' suggestion by saying that Prodicus knew what Simonides meant by the word but was jesting and merely trying to test Protagoras' ability to defend his interpretation of χαλεπόν as meaning 'not easy' in accordance with its common usage (341d7-9), it becomes clear that Socrates is making manifest Prodicus' ignorance in the very skill that the sophist claims as his own. Prodicus not only fails to understand Simonides' meaning but he also assumes Simonides was objecting to Pittacus' faulty diction caused by the latter's being from Lesbos (341c6-9). A funny twist has taken place: Prodicus, and not Simonides or Pittacus, is the one unable to distinguish between various shades of meaning: τὰ ὀνόματα οὐκ ἠπίστατο ὀρθῶς διαιρεῖν—'he does not know to distinguish meanings correctly' (341c7-8).

Socrates, agreeing with Protagoras, provides another line from the Simonidean poem as proof that Simonides could not have meant χαλεπόν in the sense of κακόν. He says to Protagoras:

ἐπεὶ ὅτι γε Σιμωνίδης οὐ λέγει τὸ χαλεπὸν κακόν, μέγα τεκμήριόν ἐστιν εὐθὺς τὸ μετὰ τοῦτο ῥῆμα· λέγει γὰρ ὅτι--
  θεὸς ἂν μόνος τοῦτ' ἔχοι γέρας,
οὐ δήπου τοῦτό γε λέγων, κακὸν ἐσθλὸν ἔμμεναι, εἶτα τὸν θεόν φησιν μόνον τοῦτο ἂν ἔχειν καὶ τῷ θεῷ τοῦτο γέρας ἀπένειμε μόνῳ.

(341d9-e6)

Actually the very next words provide ample proof that Simonides did not equate 'hard' with 'bad.' He goes on,
   A god alone can have this privilege,
and presumably he does not first say 'it is bad to be noble' and then add that only a god could achieve it, and allot it as a privilege entirely divine.

According to Socrates, the line quoted immediately follows the lines of Simonides' poem mentioned by Protagoras. The γέρας in the poem of Simonides refers to the condition of being ἐσθλός (here used in place of ἀγαθός). Socrates' citing of Simonides' words about a god alone having the privilege of 'being noble' shows that he, like Protagoras, knows the poem well. His knowledge of the poem's contents becomes clearer as the dialogue progresses and it should be noted that it is Socrates (not Protagoras) who quotes other lines from Simonides' ᾆσμα ('song' or 'poem'). If Socrates later quotes lines in order to uphold his interpretation of the poet's overall intent (341e7-8: ἅ μοι δοκεῖ διανοεῖσθαι Σιμωνίδης ἐν τούτῳ τῷ ᾄσματι— 'what I think is Simonides' intention in this song'), then it is reasonable to assume that he will select only those lines in accordance with his view of the poem. More importantly, his purpose in discussing this poem in particular is to show Protagoras that he is περὶ ἐπῶν δεινός (338e7-339a1) and that he can confront Protagoras on his own terms, since, like the sophist, he is "educated" in matters relating to poetry. Protagoras claims that knowledge of poetry is the greatest part of a man's education (338e7). As a result, Socrates now is forced to display his own δεινότης ('cleverness') concerning the Simonidean poem about ἀρετή. It is striking that Socrates must give an account of virtue by being δεινός, a quality ascribed usually to sophists. If Socrates must adopt the sophistry of a Protagoras in order to take up the latter's challenge, then the seemingly awkward argumentation of Socrates is intended to be understood as a feeble attempt on the philosopher's part to resemble a sophist. I venture to suggest that Plato intended Socrates' arguments not to be persuasive; Socrates must not play by the rules of Protagoras' game.

If Protagoras forces Socrates to pose as a literary critic in the mode of a sophist like Protagoras,[9] then it is not surprising that the philosopher would resort to an interpretation of Simonides' poem that allows for amplification of the views of Socrates the philosopher and not Socrates the Protagorean-style critic of poetry. In fact, Socrates focuses on philosophical questions

---

9. See 338e6-339a3 for Protagoras' opinion on what it means to be περὶ ἐπῶν δεινός.

concerning ontology (more precisely, the difference between 'becoming' and 'being' in the lines of Simonides and Pittacus, respectively) and his own famous contention that "no one errs willingly," a view he ascribes to Simonides and the other wise men (345d9-e2: οὐδεὶς τῶν σοφῶν ἀνδρῶν ἡγεῖται οὐδένα ἀνθρώπων ἑκόντα ἐξαμαρτάνειν—'no wise man thinks anyone errs willingly').

Socrates begins his interpretation of Simonides' poem at 342a6. Before quoting various lines, he prefaces his monologue with a small excursus on Crete and Sparta as the oldest leading centers of philosophy in Hellas. Sophists, he goes on to say, abound in these areas but they, like the sophists whom Protagoras had mentioned earlier (316d2-317c1), deny being sophists and hide their wisdom (342b1-6). These Cretan and Spartan "sophists" are so protective of their *sophia* that they pretend that their regions excel rather in warfare and courage so as not to share their wisdom with others (342b4-6). Socrates is obviously parodying Protagoras' earlier comments about the reluctance of the sophists of old to divulge their being sophists; Protagoras, on the other hand, is not afraid to show his knowledge. Socrates' purpose in this part of the *Protagoras* is obvious: to mock Protagoras' style of exposition as displayed in his earlier discussion about his relationship to the ancients and to contrast Protagoras' μακρολογία ('speaking at length')[10] with the Laconic brevity of Pittacus' maxim as quoted by Simonides. Socrates contends that the Spartans have the best education with respect to philosophy and *logoi*. According to Socrates, the ability to utter short remarks that become memorable sayings is the hallmark of education, and he counts Pittacus of Mytilene as one of the traditional seven sages[11] who were influenced by Spartan *paideia*. He attributes maxims like γνῶθι σαυτόν ('know thyself') and μηδὲν ἄγαν ('nothing in excess') to these

---

10. Cf. 334c8-335c7 for Socrates' complaint against Protagoras' μακροὶ λόγοι. Parry 1965.318-320 provides a discussion of the theme of *makrologia* as found in the *Protagoras* along with a conjecture "that a disparagement of the *makros logos* occurred somewhere in Simonides' poem" (p. 320).

11. 343a1-b3 is the earliest extant reference to a list of seven sages whose membership varies in the ancient sources. See *RE* s.v. "Die Sieben Weisen" for other extant references.

disciples of Spartan culture and then proceeds to classify Pittacus' remark that it is difficult to be noble (as mentioned by Simonides) as an example of these pithy "philosophical" statements.

According to Socrates, Simonides intended to 'take down' (343c1: καθέλοι) Pittacus' gnomic statement because he, covetous of fame, wished to gain a reputation for wisdom.[12] Simonides' entire poem then is a refutation of Pittacus' gnome (343c3-5 and 344b3-5). Socrates' account of Simonides' motivation indirectly mocks the practice of sophists like Protagoras who hope to debunk traditional wisdom in order to display their own cleverness. Although Socrates' tone seems not altogether serious, his detailed analysis of the poem suggests that he is intent upon clearing Simonides of self-contradiction. Surely Protagoras' opinion regarding the poem must have been novel; otherwise, Socrates would not have been compelled to defend Simonides. The arguments that Socrates provides, however, are at times strained and, as we shall see, skewed toward Socratic preoccupations.

To support his assertion that Simonides finds fault with Pittacus' maxim regarding virtue, Socrates points to the μέν in the first line quoted by Protagoras and regards it as an indication that Simonides disagrees with the subsequent lines containing Pittacus' maxim (343d1-6). One cannot know whether this interpretation is correct, since the lines that came between the two quotations presented by Protagoras are missing. A corresponding δέ clause that is not available to us may have provided the key to understanding Simonides' intent. Although some scholars find Socrates' treatment of the μέν clause unconvincing,[13] it is a possible interpretation if one accepts Socrates' insistence upon the difference between Pittacus' χαλεπὸν

---

12. Protagoras also can be described as φιλότιμος...ἐπὶ σοφίᾳ (343c1) when he charges Simonides with self-contradiction. As Woodbury 1953.137 points out, the sophists customarily tried to subvert the authority of the poets by arguing that their views were self-contradictory.

13. Taylor 1991.145, for example, views Socrates' interpretation here as not impossible—i.e., Socrates understands the lines to mean "it is rather (*men*) becoming good which is difficult, not (*de*) being good"—but finds it as strained as the immediately following treatment of ἀληθῶς (343d6-344a6).

ἐσθλὸν ἔμμεναι and Simonides' ἄνδρ' ἀγαθὸν γενέc χαλεπόν.¹⁴ However, his claim at 343d6-344a6 that Simon ~es used ἀλαθέως as a hyperbaton, modifying χαλεπόν rather than referring back to ἀγαθόν, seems strained and unconvincing.¹⁵ First, the natural sense of the word order precludes one's understanding 'it is truly difficult (344a4: χαλεπὸν ἀλαθέως) for a man to be good' instead of 'it is difficult for a man to be truly good'. Second, the latter meaning seems more appropriate, since Simonides expands upon the meaning of ἀγαθός in the phrase χερσίν τε καὶ ποσὶ καὶ νόῳ τετράγωνον, ἄνευ ψόγου τετυγμένον ('hands and feet and mind foursquare, wrought without blame').¹⁶

Instead of claiming that Socrates misunderstands Simonides, it is better to consider Socrates' motivation during this segment of his analysis. In the case of the alleged hyperbaton, clearly he is trying, at any cost, to maintain that Simonides does not contradict himself. Socrates' maneuver at 343e-344a is sophistic— i.e., clever but fallacious. More precisely, his is an obviously clumsy attempt at "Protagorean" argumentation. One can view the allusion to μακρολογία at 344b, a practice already attributed to Protagoras by Socrates (334c9-d1) and Alcibiades (336c5-6), as another ironic reference to Protagoras' argumentative style; Socrates says that he will not delve into all the intricacies of the

---

14. Cf. Frede 1986.740-41. Wilamowitz 1913.165, however, found no difference in meaning between Simonides' γενέσθαι and Pittacus' ἔμμεναι. Socrates had made the distinction already at 340c4-7.

15. See Taylor 1991.145 and Donlan 1969.79 for dismissals of Socrates' assertions. Frede 1986.740-41 defends Socrates "rather implausible claim" as a "tortuous reading...designed to stress the distinction between 'becoming good' and 'being good'."

16. Cf. Arist. Nic. Ethic. 1100b20-22: τὰς τύχας οἴσει κάλλιστα καὶ πάντῃ πάντως ἐμμελῶς ὅ γ' ὡς ἀληθῶς ἀγαθὸς καὶ τετράγωνος ἄνευ ψόγου (a probable allusion to Simonides' poem). Cf. also Rhet. 1411b26 for another reference to the 'foursquare' man. Gregory Nagy has brought it to my attention that the adjective 'foursquare' has an analogue in the "symmetrically" sculpted kouroi-figures of the archaic period whose bodies stand in a rigid position on a squarish plane (cf. Svenbro 1976.154ff. and Gentili 1988.255). See Rodis-Lewis 1983.274 for a similar observation: "le couros du Musée d'Agrigente, solide et net, n'évoque-t-il pas le vers de Simonide: 'L'homme vraiment bon est carré de corps et d'esprit?'"

well-wrought poem, since it would take up too much time (344b2-3: ἀλλὰ μακρὸν ἂν εἴη αὐτὸ οὕτω διελθεῖν). Even though he promises to provide an 'outline' (τύπον) of the poem and a discussion of its overall 'purpose' (βούλησιν) as a 'refutation' (ἔλεγχος)[17] of Pittacus' saying, his subsequent analysis is lengthy. Socrates' presentation can then be understood as a subtle mimicry of the sophists infused with a serious purpose. He feels obliged to defend Simonides from the charge of self-contradiction. The convoluted defense, as will be shown, also becomes an opportunity for Socrates to voice his own philosophical views although they are attributed to Simonides.[18] If one sees Socrates' attempt at literary criticism in such a light, then his interpretation does not seem so outlandish.

At 334b6-c5, Socrates reiterates what he has just argued, emphasizing that Simonides says 'it is truly difficult to become a good man' as though the poet were defending a thesis (344b6-7: ὡς ἂν εἰ λέγοι λόγον). However, the poet's contention is now expanded upon by Socrates, who claims that Simonides regards 'becoming *agathos*' as possible only for a short period. The distinction between 'becoming good' (Simonides) and 'being in a state of goodness' (Pittacus) is mentioned again and thus introduces Socrates' next comment, which he imagines Simonides himself would say if the poet were addressing Pittacus. Simonides would assert that it is not possible for human beings 'to be good'[19] since this is a privilege assigned only to the gods.[20] He quotes additional lines from the poem that presumably followed the phrase referring to the gods' γέρας:

---

17. Socrates' diction here is noteworthy. He uses a term usually found in the context of philosophy to describe the motivation of a lyric poet such as Simonides.

18. For the most part, I share the opinion of Frede 1986.737: "apart from the comic (and sometimes, admittedly, silly) elements, I want to maintain that Socrates' interpretation of Simonides is basically sound (with some other commentators) and contains some important Socratic/Platonic tenets...." Giuliano 1991 also offers a sympathetic treatment of Socrates' philosophical, rather than philological, exegesis.

19. *Agathos* is used in lieu of Pittacus' *esthlos*. See note 27 below.

20. It is not clear from the text whether Socrates is paraphrasing or incorrectly requoting the line he mentioned in 341e2. Cf. Arist. *Metaph.* A 982b29.

ἄνδρα δ' οὐκ ἔστι μὴ οὐ κακὸν ἔμμεναι,
ὃν [ἂν] ἀμήχανος συμφορὰ καθέλῃ.
(344c4-5)

He cannot but be bad, whom once
Helpless disaster casts down.

This is followed by Socrates' insistence that these lines refer to the man who is at times εὐμήχανος ('resourceful'), not to the man who is always ἀμήχανος ('helpless'). He uses a quintessentially Socratic technique here: the comparison of those with the knowledge of some craft (e.g., sailors, farmers, doctors, etc.) to those who profess to have ἀρετή. The meaning of ἀμήχανος συμφορά here is obvious in the context of these lines. 'Helpless disaster'[21] refers to circumstances beyond a man's control that render him κακός.[22] Socrates, in a clever play on words, contends that the εὐμήχανος man would be the only one susceptible to ἀμήχανος συμφορά (344d1-2).[23] The argumentation provided here seems pointless; however, it can be considered a feeble attempt at defending the upshot of this part of his presentation. His purpose is to defend Simonides' statement that 'it is difficult to become ἀγαθός' and to infer that the poet would adduce that 'it is impossible to be good'. If misfortune especially attacks the resourceful man, as Socrates alleges, then it can be argued (albeit dubiously) that only a good man can become κακός while the κακός man is κακός always.[24]

Socrates quotes from another poet, unknown to us, whose views resemble those of Simonides': αὐτὰρ ἀνὴρ ἀγαθὸς τοτὲ

---

21. Cf. Taylor 1991.146 for a discussion of the two meanings of this phrase.

22. The argument of Donlan (1969.82-83) claiming that κακός and ἀμήχανος συμφορά are both "moral" terms is unconvincing. His translation of the latter as "a natural defect of human nature" (p. 83) goes beyond the demands of the poem's context.

23. Note Socrates' transference of the adjective ἀμήχανος to refer to the 'resourceless' victim (344d2-4).

24. Socrates makes this clear in 345b5-8: ὁ δὲ κακὸς ἀνὴρ οὐκ ἄν ποτε γένοιτο κακός - ἔστιν γὰρ ἀεί - ἀλλ' εἰ μέλλει κακὸς γενέσθαι, δεῖ αὐτὸν πρότερον ἀγαθὸν γενέσθαι.

μὲν κακός, ἄλλοτε δ' ἐσθλός—'a good man is sometimes bad, sometimes noble' (344d8).[25] Simonides would say 'to become good is difficult but possible'. The assertion that 'to be good' (ἐσθλὸν ἔμμεναι) is not possible—at least for human beings— is re-emphasized.[26] Another quotation from Simonides' poem is added as further evidence for Socrates' interpretation:

πράξας μὲν γὰρ εὖ πᾶς ἀνὴρ ἀγαθός,
κακὸς δ' εἰ κακῶς.

(344e7-8)

For when he fares well every man is good,
But in ill faring, evil.

The subsequent discussion of these lines allows Socrates to interject one of his favorite philosophical tenets, the notion that 'doing badly' (κακὴ πρᾶξις) consists only of 'being deprived of knowledge' (ἐπιστήμης στερηθῆναι).[27] This transition at 345b5 to Socrates' familiar claim regarding the relationship between virtue and knowledge is abrupt; however, one should not discard it on the grounds of seeming irrelevance. On the contrary, it offers a glimpse of Socrates' insistence on the truth of his own beliefs regarding the nature of virtue.

He manages to connect Simonides' notion that being κακός is a product of external forces that a man cannot overcome with his own conception of 'doing badly' applied to a man's "inner" state comprised of knowledge.[28] Socrates achieves the fusion of

---

25. This is a hexameter line. The thought herein reminds one of gnomological poetry, especially Hesiod and Theognis.

26. Cf. 344c1-3 to 344e4-6 (a hypothetical conversation between Simonides and Pittacus provides the setting for the vocative ὦ Πιττακέ found in these two passages).

27. See Frede 1986.742-43 for a useful discussion of this passage (345a-b).

28. For a different view of Simonides' meaning, see Donlan 1969.83: "The poet says in effect that these words [*agathos-esthlos, kakos*] should no longer be used to describe man in his external fortunes, but rather in terms of his internal worth." The *Theognidea* clearly demonstrates that these words can apply to both the character of a man (i.e., his "internal" state) and his

these views by likening the plight of a ship's pilot and a farmer, both susceptible to nature's forces (344d), to the κακὴ πρᾶξις of a doctor who, unlike 'laymen' (ἰδιῶται), possesses a certain type of knowledge (345a-b). Since no one has absolute knowledge, no one can be ἀγαθός always. One cannot be sure that Simonides shared Socrates' philosophical tenet; however, Socrates does agree with the poet's attitude regarding the fragility of human goodness. Socrates interprets Simonides as implying that in order to become 'bad', one must first become 'good' (345b7-8). Socrates' wording here is important because he clearly states that his interpretation is what Simonides had intended (345b8: ὥστε καὶ τοῦτο τοῦ ᾄσματος πρὸς τοῦτο τείνει...). In other words, Socrates is carrying Simonides' poem a step further than the poet had. It is not clear from the context whether the phrase at 345c3 (ἐπὶ πλεῖστον δὲ καὶ ἄριστοί εἰσιν οὓς ἂν οἱ θεοὶ φιλῶσιν—'those are best for the longest time whom the gods love') is Socrates' paraphrase of a line from the poem or the actual words of Simonides.[29]

Socrates continues to quote from the poem:

τοὔνεκεν οὔ ποτ' ἐγὼ τὸ μὴ γενέσθαι δυνατὸν
διζήμενος κενεὰν ἐς ἄπρακτον ἐλπίδα μοῖραν αἰῶνος
    βαλέω,
πανάμωμον ἄνθρωπον, εὐρυεδοῦς ὅσοι καρπὸν αἰνύμεθα
    χθονός·
ἐπὶ θ' ὑμῖν εὑρὼν ἀπαγγελέω.

(345c6-11)

Then never shall I vainly cast away
In hopeless search my little share of life,
Seeking a thing impossible to be,
A man all blameless, among those who reap
The fruit of the broad earth. But should I find him
I'll send you word.

---

social status determined by the possession of external qualities such as courage, good looks, and wealth.

29. The phrase appears in small type in *PMG* 542 (lines 19-20).

Although Socrates quotes these lines as additional support for his argument that Simonides is attacking Pittacus, he does not discuss their meaning immediately; he postpones his interpretation until later (at 346d). Simonides' words are similar to what one finds in praise/blame poetry. The adjective παν-άμωμος ('utterly blameless'), a *hapax legomenon*, probably is synonymous with the earlier description of the 'foursquare' man as one who is 'fashioned without blame' (ἄνευ ψόγου τετυγ-μένος).[30] A Semonides fragment contains the adjective ἄμωμος modified by the adverb πάμπαν, and, as M. Dickie has noted, the sense in which Semonides uses it is the same as Simonides' πανάμωμος.[31] Both poets state that a totally blameless human being does not exist. Simonides' tone seems cynical in the last line, since it is probable that he will not be able to find such a man.[32]

The claim that Simonides directs his poem against the saying of Pittacus is repeated, and, in what appears as an anacolouthon,[33] he quickly shifts to quoting more lines as supposed evidence for this view of Simonides' motivation:

πάντας δ' ἐπαίνημι καὶ φιλέω
ἑκὼν ὅστις ἔρδῃ
μηδὲν αἰσχρόν· ἀνάγκῃ δ' οὐδὲ θεοὶ μάχονται.

---

30. Note the emphatic position of the adjective (used at the beginning of the line). Another cognate of μέμφομαι occurs at 346c (φιλόμωμος). Socrates quotes Simonides who refuses to blame a ὑγιὴς ἀνήρ (346c4-5): οὔ μιν ἐγὼ μωμήσομαι.

31. Cf. Semonides, fr. 4 W: πάμπαν δ' ἄμωμος οὔ τις οὐδ' ἀκήριος. A discussion of its meaning in relation to Simonides' poem is offered by Dickie 1978.23-24. Along with Dickie, I think that "Simonides does no more than give expression to the common Greek belief that no man is fortunate in all respects" (p. 24) in the lines quoted by Socrates.

32. The text at 345c11 is uncertain. Burnet's edition of the *Protagoras* has ἐπὶ θ' at 345c11 and 346d5 while two of the manuscripts (B, T) contain ἔπειθ'. Page 1962 emends the manuscripts' reading *metri causa* to ἐπὶ δ' ὑμίν.

33. 345d1-2 (οὕτω σφόδρα καὶ δι' ὅλου τοῦ ᾄσματος ἐπεξέρχεται τῷ τοῦ Πιττακοῦ ῥήματι). Cf. 345d6 (καὶ τοῦτ' ἐστὶ πρὸς τὸ αὐτὸ τοῦτο εἰρημένον) for further repetition of what is said at 345c4-5 (and previously at 344b4-5).

(345d3-5)

But all who do no baseness willingly
I praise and love. The gods themselves strive not
Against necessity.

Another abrupt transition occurs; this time, however, it is shifted toward another of Socrates' own philosophical views. As before (cf. 345b5), he ascribes one of his philosophical tenets to Simonides. His belief that "no one errs willingly" finds a place in the subsequent interpretation of these lines. According to Socrates, Simonides was not so uneducated (ἀπαίδευτος) as to believe 'that there were some who performed evil deeds willingly' (345d6-9). He cleverly reintroduces the 'wise men' at this point and attributes his (Socrates') belief to them: [οἱ σοφοὶ ἄνδρες] εὖ ἴσασιν ὅτι πάντες οἱ τὰ αἰσχρὰ καὶ τὰ κακὰ ποιοῦντες ἄκοντες ποιοῦσιν—'they know well that all who do shameful and bad things do them unwillingly' (345e2-4). In light of this belief supposedly shared by Simonides and the other wise men,[34] Socrates asserts that the adjective ἑκών refers to Simonides himself and not to the relative clause ὅστις ἔρδῃ μηδὲν αἰσχρόν. Although the natural word order would preclude Socrates' interpretation, his claim is repeated later at 346e1-4 where Socrates says that Simonides uses ἐπαίνημι, the 'Mytilenaean' form of ἐπαινῶ, because the phrase beginning 'I love and praise all willingly' is addressed to Pittacus, who is a native of Mytilene.[35]

The curious aspect of Socrates' analysis in 346a-b is that he not only inserts his own philosophical view but also concentrates on a topic whose relevance is not immediately understood. He dwells on the subject of the tendency of 'wicked men' (οἱ πονηροί) to delight in finding fault with the wrongdoing of relatives or others, whereas 'good men' (οἱ ἀγαθοί) force themselves, by means of reconciliation and exhortation, 'to love and

---

34. As Taylor 1991.147 points out, "Socrates' claim that his thesis is universally accepted is ironical, as it was generally regarded as outrageously implausible (e.g., *Gorg.* 475e)."

35. Since Aeolic forms are not uncommon in Greek lyric, Socrates' explanation of Simonides' rationale seems somewhat "tongue in cheek."

praise' those who act unjustly (e.g., their own parents or homeland).[36] Note that Socrates is sneaking in his own view of the way one should behave toward one's family and country. Perhaps he is also paying Simonides a backhanded compliment, since the poet, as Socrates says,[37] found himself in circumstances that compelled him to bestow praise upon such figures as tyrants; Simonides would then be counted as one of the ἀγαθοί who do not easily find fault with anyone.[38] It is important for Socrates to note that Simonides, like the 'good' men, felt at times that he was praising under the force of necessity (346b7: ἀναγκαζόμενος), 'not willingly' (οὐχ ἑκών).

After the lengthy digression on 'loving and praising', Socrates provides more lines from the poem in a convoluted juxtaposition of quotation and paraphrase:[39]

ταῦτα δὴ καὶ τῷ Πιττακῷ λέγει ὅτι Ἐγώ, ὦ Πιττακέ, οὐ
διὰ ταῦτά σε ψέγω, ὅτι εἰμὶ φιλόψογος, ἐπεί--

---

36. An ironical foreshadowing of the Simonidean phrase linking praise and love (employed by Socrates throughout 346a-b) occurs at 335e when Socrates says to Callias that he 'now praises and loves' (νῦν ἐπαινῶ καὶ φιλῶ) the latter's love of learning.

37. See 346b5-8.

38. Although Frede 1986.746 interprets Socrates' intent as mischievous insofar as he is mocking encomiastic poets, I am reluctant to dismiss the significance of his elaborate disquisition on praise and blame in the passage under discussion. Perhaps Socrates is doing more than just mocking Simonides since he turns this indirect attack against Simonides on its head and employs it in defense of the poet. Socrates may be serious when he states that 'good' men do not blame those who wrong them. His opinions regarding his relationship to the laws of Athens in the *Crito* resemble what he interprets as Simonides' own belief regarding the ideal behavior of the καλὸς κἀγαθός (cf. 345e6-346a3). Even though Socrates appears to attack poets like Simonides because they praised tyrants, at the same time he is attributing his own notion of ideal conduct to the poet. In other words, I do not think that this passage is meant only as an indictment of Simonides; Socrates again insinuates his own "philosophy" here.

39. It is unclear which words are Socrates' and which belong to Simonides' poem. Page, for example, in *PMG* 542 adds his own conjecture inserting οὐκ εἰμὶ φιλόψογος as a clause preceding ἐπεί (understood as part of the poem) ἔμοιγε ἐξαρκεῖ. In addition, he prints †μὴν† rather than Schleiermacher's conjecture, μιν.

ἔμοιγ' ἐξαρκεῖ ὃς ἂν μὴ κακὸς ᾖ
μηδ' ἄγαν ἀπάλαμνος, εἰδώς τ' ὀνησίπολιν
    δίκαν ὑγιὴς ἀνήρ·
    οὔ μιν ἐγὼ μωμήσομαι--
οὐ γάρ εἰμι φιλόμωμος--
    τῶν γὰρ ἠλιθίων ἀπείρων γενέθλα,
ὥστ' εἴ τις χαίρει ψέγων, ἐμπλησθείη ἂν ἐκείνους
μεμφόμενος--
    πάντα τοι καλά, τοῖσί τ' αἰσχρὰ μὴ μέμεικται.
                                        (346b8-c11)

This then is addressed to Pittacus in particular, as if to say, My reason for blaming you, Pittacus, is not that I am a faultfinder, for
> to me that man suffices
> Who is not bad nor overweak, but sound
> In heart and knowing righteousness, the weal
> Of nations. I shall find no fault with him—

I am not, he says, a censorious man—
> For beyond number is the tribe of fools.

So, he implies, if anyone takes pleasure in faultfinding, he may have his fill in censuring them.
> All is fair that is unmixed with foul.

These lines, according to the Socratic interpretation, are directed at Pittacus (cf. 347a1-3). One should not rule out the possibility that they actually refer to Scopas, the addressee of the poem (as mentioned by Protagoras in 339a7). The meaning of the adjective ἀπάλαμνος here is a matter of scholarly debate, since it can mean 'helpless, good for naught' or 'reckless, lawless'.[40] Although some understand the word in the latter sense,[41] the con-

---

40. See *LSJ* s.v. 'ἀπάλαμνος' for references.
41. For example, Wilamowitz 1913.175 considers it synonymous with ὑβριστής. Taylor 1991.147 argues that 'wicked' is a better translation than 'helpless' because it "fits the context better, esp. the contrast with justice." I think it contrasts just as easily with the adjective qualifying 'justice': ὀνησίπολις.

## Protagoras 31

sensus maintains that it does not have a "moral" overtone.[42] The word recalls the sense of the adjective ἀμήχανος used earlier by Simonides to describe συμφορά (344c5). Moreover, it would be appropriate for it to mean 'ineffectual', since it is contrasted with the adjective ὑγιής ('sound' in body and mind)[43] that characterizes a 'man who knows justice which benefits the *polis*'. Simonides' words are reminiscent of the poetry of Solon and Theognis; both are concerned with the preservation of *dikê* in the city-state. Unfortunately, one cannot be sure of Simonides' train of thought because Socrates may be quoting lines that, out of context, can fit into his own interpretation as offered in 346d1-347a5.

The final part of Socrates' interpretation briefly refers to the last line quoted (πάντα τοι καλά, τοῖσί τ' αἰσχρὰ μὴ μέμεικται ('all is fair that is unmixed with foul').[44] Simonides, he says, is expressing here his allowance for the middle state (namely, the poet's acceptance of actions not completely καλά, but still not 'shameful') as free from reproach: τὰ μέσα ἀποδέχεται ὥστε μὴ ψέγειν (346d3).[45] After a rapid repetition of the lines quoted earlier regarding the 'utterly blameless man', the upshot of Simonides' words is provided in a hodgepodge of requotation and exegesis (346d-e). Simonides is understood to

---

42. Woodbury 1953.161 offers convincing arguments for its meaning 'helpless' rather than 'wrongful'. Unlike Donlan 1969.89, I do not think that "Simonides is referring to a state of moral helplessness."

43. Although this may be the earliest use of ὑγιής in the sense of 'sound in mind' (cf. Taylor 1991.147), it is possible that Simonides meant both physical and mental soundness in the context since the first lines quoted by Protagoras refer to a man's being 'foursquare in hands, feet, and mind'.

44. Cf. Pindar fr. 181 Snell-Maehler for a similar notion that praise can become 'mixed' into blame: ὁ γὰρ ἐξ οἴκου ποτὶ μῶμον ἔπαινος κίρναται.

45. Worthy of note is Socrates' use of τὰ μέσα to designate average behavior. Although the theme of following the mean is common enough (cf. Theognis 335-336: πάντων μέσ' ἄριστα, followed, incidentally, by this statement to Kurnos which recalls the first lines quoted from Simonides' poem: καὶ οὕτως,/ Κύρν', ἕξεις ἀρετήν, ἥντε λαβεῖν χαλεπόν), it would be in keeping with the geometrical terminology already employed in the poem (cf. 'foursquare') if Socrates used the phrase here in its sense as "the mean terms in a proportion." The proportion under discussion would then be one of what is considered τὰ καλά and what is not.

mean that he is content if a man is 'average' (μέσος) and does nothing κακόν. This is followed by the reassertion that the adjective ἑκών should refer to Simonides' act of loving and praising whoever does nothing αἰσχρόν.[46] Then, still speaking as though he were the poet, Socrates feebly appends a comment on having to praise against one's will: ἄκων δ' ἔστιν οὓς ἐγὼ ἐπαινῶ καὶ φιλῶ (346e3-4: 'there are those whom I praise and love against my will'). The hypothetical scenario continues with Simonides blaming Pittacus for pretending to tell the truth when in fact the latter is 'grievously lying about matters of the greatest importance' (347a2-3).[47] Socrates had just claimed that Simonides does not consider himself φιλόψογος ('fond of blaming'), since, in the poet's words, 'the race (γενέθλα) of fools is endless' and one could have one's fill of blaming them. Obviously, Socrates has not quoted line by line here; consequently, it is difficult to reconstruct the context in which the quotations occur. All that can be said is that Socrates has concentrated on Simonides himself and has insisted that the poet blames Pittacus, even though Simonides, in his own words, says that he usually does not like to find fault with others. It is hard to believe that anyone would have taken Simonides' claim seriously, since a major function of poetry is to offer praise (especially in epinician poetry and throughout Greek poetry in general) and blame. Therefore, Socrates may be pretending to accept Simonides' pose in order to highlight his contention that Simonides, one who was not φιλόμωμος, felt obliged to blame Pittacus for not telling the truth. Turning to Prodicus and Protagoras, Socrates finishes his exegesis: ταῦτά μοι δοκεῖ... Σιμωνίδης διανοούμενος πεποιηκέναι τοῦτο τὸ ᾆσμα (347a3-5: 'this is what I think Simonides intended in the making of his poem').

---

46. Note that Socrates seems inconsistent in his terminology. However, I do not think that the point he is making, even if it is unsubstantiated, should be discarded on the grounds of faulty logic. Rather, it should be regarded in the context of a clumsy Socratic attempt to be "sophistic."

47. Socrates claims that Simonides would say to Pittacus: σὲ οὖν, καὶ εἰ μέσως ἔλεγες ἐπιεικῆ καὶ ἀληθῆ, ὦ Πιττακέ, οὐκ ἄν ποτε ἔψεγον (346e4-347a1). The use of the adverb μέσως here is part of Socrates' attempt to give cohesion to his interpretation; cf. 346d3-7 for references to 'middle' states.

## Protagoras 33

Hippias, another sophist who figures prominently in the *Protagoras*, commends Socrates for his interpretation. Hippias' words are important because they do not refer to Socrates' interpretation alone; Hippias himself says that he too has a fine λόγος ('interpretation') regarding the Simonidean poem he is willing to display "on the spot" to the immediate audience. This reference to another possible interpretation of the poem is significant because it implies that Socrates' immediate audience thought that a poem could be viewed in many different ways. More importantly, if a 'poem' (ᾆσμα) is subject to more than one λόγος and each of these λόγοι can be considered equally 'good',[48] then Socrates' interpretation should not be dismissed as an unsound display of literary criticism. On the contrary, Simonides' poem provides Protagoras and Socrates the opportunity to provide differing but acceptable accounts of a work known to their listeners. One of these listeners, the sophist Hippias, has another view of Simonides' poem, and this implies that the art of exegesis is not rigid in the eyes of Plato's intended audience. Various interpretations can be offered for one poem and none of them is absolutely correct, even if one interpretation seems to possess more δεινότης than another. Consequently, in the eyes of his audience, Socrates' exegesis would be considered one of many possible interpretations of Simonides' poem.

This is a significant observation, since Socrates' interpretation has been the subject of debate for generations of scholars who have tried to make sense of the poem itself from the quotations and commentary presented by Protagoras and Socrates. Moreover, Socrates' statements regarding the poet's meaning have seemed farfetched if not openly misleading to the reader. It is doubtful that Plato's audience would have reacted to Socrates' interpretation in a manner similar to ours, since it was not uncommon for a poem to have more than one applicable λόγος. Hippias' words may serve as a kind of vindication of Socrates' views in light of the acceptance of multiple interpretations of a familiar poem by the Greeks of the fifth century B.C.E.

---

48. Hippias' words as quoted by Plato demonstrate this notion that more than one interpretation of an ᾆσμα is plausible if not equally 'good' (347a7-b2: ἔστιν μέντοι, ἔφη, καὶ ἐμοὶ λόγος περὶ αὐτοῦ εὖ ἔχων, ὃν ὑμῖν ἐπιδείξω, ἂν βούλησθε).

Hippias, however, is prevented by Alcibiades from embarking on another excursus regarding the poem. The latter curtly says 'thank you Hippias, but some other time' (347b2: ναί...εἰς αὖθις γε) and insists that the question-and-answer session between Protagoras and Socrates continue; the role of questioner can be played by either party. Although Socrates pretends to let Protagoras decide which of the two should ask the questions,[49] he steers the conversation away from poetry and back to his original question regarding the unity of the virtues (justice, holiness, temperance, etc.) under the single heading of ἀρετή (cf. 329c2-d2). Before abandoning the topic of poetry, he provides a long speech on the inappropriateness of discussing poetry in a sympotic setting of well-educated gentlemen. He compares discussions involving poetry to the gatherings or *symposia* of 'vulgar men from the marketplace' (οἱ φαῦλοι καὶ ἀγοραῖοι ἄνθρωποι) and contrasts these *symposia* to the 'gatherings' (συνουσίαι) of 'well-educated gentlemen' (καλοὶ κἀγαθοί):

> καὶ γὰρ δοκεῖ μοι τὸ περὶ ποιήσεως διαλέγεσθαι ὁμοιότατον εἶναι τοῖς συμποσίοις τοῖς τῶν φαύλων καὶ ἀγοραίων ἀνθρώπων. καὶ γὰρ οὗτοι, διὰ τὸ μὴ δύνασθαι ἀλλήλοις δι' ἑαυτῶν συνεῖναι ἐν τῷ πότῳ μηδὲ διὰ τῆς ἑαυτῶν φωνῆς καὶ τῶν λόγων τῶν ἑαυτῶν ὑπὸ ἀπαιδευσίας, τιμίας ποιοῦσι τὰς αὐλητρίδας, πολλοῦ μισθούμενοι ἀλλοτρίαν φωνὴν τὴν τῶν αὐλῶν, καὶ διὰ τῆς ἐκείνων φωνῆς ἀλλήλοις σύνεισιν· ὅπου δὲ καλοὶ κἀγαθοὶ συμπόται καὶ πεπαιδευμένοι εἰσίν, οὐκ ἂν ἴδοις οὔτ' αὐλητρίδας οὔτε ὀρχηστρίδας οὔτε ψαλτρίας, ἀλλὰ αὐτοὺς αὐτοῖς ἱκανοὺς ὄντας συνεῖναι ἄνευ τῶν λήρων τε καὶ παιδιῶν τούτων διὰ τῆς αὐτῶν φωνῆς, λέγοντάς τε καὶ ἀκούοντας ἐν μέρει ἑαυτῶν κοσμίως, κἂν πάνυ πολὺν οἶνον πίωσιν.
>
> (347c3-e1)

Conversation about poetry reminds me too much of the wine parties of cheap and common people. Such men,

---

49. Cf. 348a6-7 for Socrates' supposed willingness to accept Protagoras as his questioner.

being too uneducated to entertain themselves as they drink by using their own voices and conversation, put up the price of female flute-players, paying well for the extraneous sound of the flutes, and associate with each other amidst the sound. But where the drinkers are men of worth and culture, you will not see flute-players, dancers or harpists. They are quite capable of enjoying their own company without such frivolous and childish things, using their own voices in sober discussion and each taking his turn to speak or listen, even if the wine-drinking is heavy.

Socrates paints a vivid picture of the sympotic environment of the 'common' men. Since they are not educated enough to entertain each other by means of intelligent conversation, they resort to hiring 'flute-girls' (347d1: αὐλητρίδας).[50] Instead of using their own words and voices, these uneducated men rely on the sound of flutes, an outside source of entertainment, while they share each other's company. He continues to contrast the two sympotic settings by emphasizing the point that educated participants have no need of these 'childish things' (347d6: παιδιῶν presumably refers to the music and dance performed by hired entertainers). They speak and listen to one another in turn while simultaneously drinking a great deal of wine.[51]

---

50. Note the scornful way in which Socrates refers to the flute-girls whom 'common' men deem worthy of honor (347c7-d1). Socrates obviously does not share their respect for entertainers hired to play music or to dance at *symposia*. Alcibiades displays a similar attitude in the *Symposium* when he refers to a flute-girl as being 'cheap' (215c4: φαύλη αὐλητρίς) in contrast to a 'virtuoso' flutist (ἀγαθὸς αὐλητής). Earlier in the same dialogue, Eryximachus dismisses a flute-girl so that the symposiasts can spend their time in conversation (176e6-9: εἰσηγοῦμαι τὴν μὲν ἄρτι εἰσελθοῦσαν αὐλητρίδα χαίρειν ἐᾶν..., ἡμᾶς δὲ διὰ λόγων ἀλλήλοις συνεῖναι τὸ τήμερον); his preference for discussion is comparable to the views offered by Socrates in the *Protagoras* regarding the proper way for educated men to behave at a similar type of gathering.

51. As Frede 1986.747 notes, Socrates' words are reminiscent of the description of the *Symposium*. However, her argument claiming that this is a deliberate reference to the *Symposium* seems unconvincing, especially because it necessitates the conjecture that Plato later added the section containing Socrates' exegesis of Simonides (and his negative comments on

Surely this type of setting is ideal for Socratic discourse; any music would be an unwelcome distraction.

The poets, says Socrates, like the extraneous sound of the flute, do not belong at a gathering such as that in the *Protagoras*. Poets cannot be questioned about their own poems and there is no consensus on how to interpret their meaning:

οὕτω δὲ καὶ αἱ τοιαίδε συνουσίαι, ἐὰν μὲν λάβωνται ἀνδρῶν οἷοίπερ ἡμῶν οἱ πολλοί φασιν εἶναι, οὐδὲν δέονται ἀλλοτρίας φωνῆς οὐδὲ ποιητῶν, οὓς οὔτε ἀνερέσθαι οἷόν τ' ἐστὶν περὶ ὧν λέγουσιν, ἐπαγόμενοί τε αὐτοὺς οἱ πολλοὶ ἐν τοῖς λόγοις οἱ μὲν ταῦτά φασιν τὸν ποιητὴν νοεῖν, οἱ δ' ἕτερα, περὶ πράγματος διαλεγόμενοι ὃ ἀδυνατοῦσι ἐξελέγξαι· ἀλλὰ τὰς μὲν τοιαύτας συνουσίας ἐῶσιν χαίρειν, αὐτοὶ δ' ἑαυτοῖς σύνεισιν δι' ἑαυτῶν, ἐν τοῖς ἑαυτῶν λόγοις πεῖραν ἀλλήλων λαμβάνοντες καὶ διδόντες.

(347e1-348a2)

In the same way gatherings like our own, if they consist of men such as most of us claim to be, call for no extraneous voices, not even of poets. No one can interrogate poets about what they say, and most often when they are introduced into the discussion some say the poet's meaning is one thing and some another, for the topic is one on which nobody can produce a conclusive argument. The best people avoid such discussions, and entertain each other from their own resources, testing one another's mettle in what they have to say themselves.

Although Socrates condemns poets (his contemporaries) in the *Apology* for not being able to explain the meaning of their own works and claims that others can discuss the poems better than the poets themselves,[52] he does not find fault with the poets in the above passage from the *Protagoras*. In this instance, he blames 'the majority' (οἱ πολλοί) who, in contrast to educated

---

discussions about poetry) to a postulated *Proto-Protagoras* in order "to stress the aporetic character of the dialogue" (p. 751).

52. Cf. *Apology* 22a8-c8.

men, refer to poets during their conversation and present different interpretations of a poet's intent (347e4-7). Clearly Socrates is alluding here to Protagoras' introduction of the Simonides poem into the current conversation. In other words, Protagoras has not behaved in a manner befitting an 'educated gentleman' (a καλὸς κἀγαθός), since he, like the vulgar majority, discusses the poets even though he is incapable of proving one way or another what the poets actually meant.

Socrates' concluding remarks about the manner in which he and Protagoras should continue their conversation is not surprising in light of his usual "dialogue" style as fashioned by Plato. The give-and-take method of argumentation among interlocutors, which he recommends in 348a2, is the familiar Socratic method of ἔλεγχος, the preferred mode of philosophical discourse. Although the term ἔλεγχος does not appear in the passage under consideration, doubtless it is what Socrates has in mind when he says that Protagoras and he should emulate men who, 'putting the poets aside, make conversation with one another by means of their own words and test the truth as well as themselves' (348a4-6). The discussion of poetry now ends and the conversation reverts to Socrates' questioning of Protagoras on the nature of ἀρετή.

Although Socrates' interpretation of the Simonides poem in the *Protagoras* can be seen as a comic interlude within an otherwise serious discussion on the nature of virtue,[53] Plato's purpose is serious, since the interpretation of the poem is not basically unsound in light of the possibility of various interpretations for a single poem. Since Socrates felt obliged to defend Simonides from Protagoras' charge of self-contradiction and since Hippias was ready but not permitted to offer another interpretation of the poem, this episode is important insofar as Plato has Socrates take advantage of the situation. Consequently, the interpretation of poetry becomes the medium for promoting philosophical tenets. When it becomes obvious that the discussion of poetry is an inadequate means of investigating

---

53. Verdam 1928.306, for example, describes this section of the dialogue in these words: "Serius esse Plato nolebat, sed ioculabatur et artem interpretandi ad absurdum deducebat. Si ita iudicabimus, locus de carmine Simonideo non absurdus erit, sed festivissimus."

not only a given poet's intent but also 'truth' (348a5: ἀλήθεια) as a whole, the Socratic preference for philosophical discourse, exemplified by the ἔλεγχος, is reconfirmed. In addition, Protagoras' sophistry becomes Socrates' target: Simonides, regardless of his poem's meaning, is given more credibility than Protagoras, the self-proclaimed teacher of ἀρετή.

# 3

## CALLICLES' QUOTATION OF PINDAR IN THE *GORGIAS**

Perhaps the most discussed quotation from lyric poetry found in Plato is the reference by Callicles in the *Gorgias* to a Pindaric poem concerned with the labors of Herakles (fr. 169a Snell-Maehler). Although Callicles quotes only five lines from the poem, it is clear that these lines, like the reference to Simonides in the *Protagoras*, are familiar to Plato's audience. As in the *Protagoras*, one of Socrates' interlocutors quotes lyric poetry in order to defend or support his own views on a particular subject. It should be noted that it is not Socrates who introduces lyric poetry into the separate discussions with Protagoras and Gorgias; his interlocutors are responsible for the initial references to lyric poetry in these two dialogues. While Protagoras makes Simonides' poem a controversial matter involving literary criticism on the part of Socrates, Callicles' reference to Pindar seems to be adduced as support for his advocacy of "the survival of the fittest" as an axiomatic truth.

What is problematic about Callicles' quotation of Pindar is not only the meaning of the lines as intended by Pindar and as interpreted by Callicles, but also the curious fact that the manuscript tradition of Plato provides a variant reading that has puzzled generations of scholars. An analysis of the quotation's context in Callicles' conversation with Socrates must be accompanied by a look at the contents of the Pindaric fragment mentioned (either by quotation, paraphrase, or a combination of

---

* Reprinted by permission of the publisher from *Harvard Studies in Classical Philology* (94), Cambridge, Mass.: Harvard University Press, copyright © 1994 by the President and Fellows of Harvard College.

both) in other ancient sources, as well as elsewhere in Plato, and partially preserved in *P. Oxy.* 2450, fr. 1. In addition, since it has been assumed that Polycrates' fictitious Κατηγορία Σωκράτους (Accusation of Socrates), supposedly countered centuries later by Libanius' Ἀπολογία Σωκράτους (Defense of Socrates), referred to the same Pindaric passage, it has been argued that the *Gorgias* and Polycrates' lost work were somehow related. The nature of their relationship is another point of scholarly contention.[1] The aim of this study is to understand the Pindaric quotation in the context of the dialogue and to determine which of the two variant readings is preferable in light of Callicles' stance in the *Gorgias*. Even though the genuine Pindaric text is attested in two other sources,[2] the reading found in the manuscripts of the *Gorgias* should not necessarily be emended. The possibility of Callicles' misquotation of Pindar is worth considering.

Callicles' discussion with Socrates in the *Gorgias* begins at 481b when he questions the latter's sincerity during the earlier exchange with Polus. Callicles finds it unbelievable that Socrates could maintain that it is better to be the victim of injustice rather than its perpetrator (cf. Socrates at 469c1-2: εἰ δ' ἀναγκαῖον εἴη ἀδικεῖν ἢ ἀδικεῖσθαι, ἑλοίμην ἂν μᾶλλον ἀδικεῖσθαι ἢ ἀδικεῖν) and that it is preferable for an evildoer to be punished rather than to escape punishment (474b: κάκιον...τὸ μὴ διδόναι δίκην τοῦ διδόναι). Socrates responds to Callicles by encouraging him to refute these tenets. If Callicles should refuse to counter Socrates' views, then Callicles forever would be at odds with himself (482b4-6).[3] Socrates now must deal

---

1. See Dodds 1959.28-29 for specific references to discussions of this topic. Grote 1994.23 has recently argued that Plato had Polycrates in mind when he wrote the *Gorgias* and that in the dialogue, "Plato is making the counter charge that it was not Socrates, but his opponents, like Callicles, who abused and made immoral use of the Greek poets."

2. Namely, the scholion on Pind. *Nem.* 9.35a and Ael. Aristid. *or.* 45 (vol. 2, 68 Dindorf with corresponding scholion in vol. 3, 408 Dindorf).

3. Socrates uses musical terminology here, likening a man to a lyre, to describe the state of being 'discordant' or 'out of tune' (482c2: ἀσύμφωνος) with oneself. His accusing Callicles of self-disagreement recalls Protagoras' attack on Simonides. However, the tone of Socrates' initial speech to Callicles is sarcastic. Note the mocking reference to Callicles' love for

with this third interlocutor who, unlike Gorgias and Polus, presents a forceful challenge not only to Socrates' views but also to conventional notions of justice.

Callicles blames Polus for acting like Gorgias. According to Callicles, Polus was driven to self-contradiction by Socrates, who cleverly alternates his line of questioning; Socrates switches from questioning on the basis of νόμος to that of φύσις and vice versa as part of his technique to force men into self-contradiction. At first, Callicles blames Polus for having felt ashamed of his own sentiments and therefore not saying what he really thought because he was afraid to disagree with Socrates' contention that it is more shameful to commit injustice rather than be a victim of it.[4] His metaphorical language describing Socrates' 'gagging' and 'tying together Polus' hands and feet' (482e1-2: ἐπεστομίσθη, συμποδισθείς) implies an attack on Socrates, not only on Polus. This attack becomes direct when Callicles charges Socrates with pretending to be concerned with 'truth' (ἀλήθεια) and deliberately tricking his interlocutors (482e2-5, 483a2-7). Next, Callicles introduces the familiar distinction between 'nature' (φύσις) and 'convention, custom' (νόμος) into his argumentation and claims that Socrates has thought up a clever trick involving these two concepts whenever he poses questions to someone (482e5-483a8). The antithesis between φύσις and νόμος appears frequently in the Greek literature of the fifth and fourth centuries.[5] Callicles is not saying anything revolutionary at this point; he is merely setting the stage for his subsequent interpretation of what is sanctioned by φύσις. The opposition between φύσις and νόμος is also reflected in the discrepancy between Polus' true sentiments and his reluctance to proclaim them.[6] One infers that φύσις somehow

---

Demos, son of Pyrilampes, and for the Athenian *demos* as compared to Socrates' own loves, Alcibiades and philosophy (481d-e).

4. Callicles follows Socrates' practice of using terms such as "worse" and "more shameful" interchangeably.

5. For a useful discussion of this topic, consult Guthrie 1969.55-134 (especially 101-107 and 131-134 treating Callicles' views and his quotation of Pindar), Heinimann 1945.110-169, and Kerferd 1981.111-130.

6. Note the repetition of ἐναντία at 482e5 and e7, which implies that a parallel is to be drawn between the two sets of antitheses.

corresponds to Polus' view of reality while νόμος, designating 'the general consensus', impedes his stating this view.

Callicles' little regard for conventional attitudes has already appeared in a preceding statement identifying 'what is fine by convention, not by nature' (482e4-5: ἃ φύσει μὲν οὐκ ἔστιν καλά, νόμῳ δέ) with 'base and low arguments aimed at the public' (482e3-4: φορτικὰ καὶ δημηγορικά). These words show that Callicles considers his views superior to those of the οἱ πολλοί. His choice of words characterizes him as someone who sets himself apart from society and its conventions and foreshadows the *Weltanschauung* he will espouse. He takes pains to distinguish himself from Socrates also, especially since the latter is 'misbehaving' (483a2-3: κακουργεῖς) by sometimes asking questions on the basis of νόμος, at other times on the basis of φύσις, and thereby ensnaring those responding to his questions in a trap of self-contradiction. Whenever someone talks on the basis of 'convention', Socrates questions him on the basis of 'nature' and vice versa. Callicles sees Socrates' exchange with Polus as an example of the use of this sly technique that operates between two supposedly antithetical spheres. Beginning at 483a7, Callicles unfolds his understanding of the difference between φύσις and its opposite.

According to Callicles, 'suffering wrong' (483a8: τὸ ἀδικεῖσθαι) is worse and more shameful 'by nature' (φύσει), whereas, 'by convention' (νόμῳ), 'doing wrong' (τὸ ἀδικεῖν) is the greater evil.[7] 'Suffering wrong' is experienced only by slaves who are unable to help themselves and others in their care when they are wronged and abused. He thinks that weak men, the majority of the populace, laid down the 'laws' (νόμοι), since these laws are to their advantage (483b4-7).[8] In order to frighten stronger men and prevent them from 'overreaching' (πλέον ἔχειν), the weak men say that it is shameful and unjust to 'overreach' and that 'doing wrong' consists in seeking to have more than what others have: λέγουσιν ὡς αἰσχρὸν καὶ ἄδικον

---

7. The views expressed here by Callicles are similar to those of Antiphon the Sophist regarding νόμος versus φύσις (Diels-Kranz 87 B 44).

8. Callicles here seems to be conflating the various meanings of νόμος. 'Law' and 'convention' are the same thing in this context insofar as 'laws' are formal encodings of what is prescribed by 'convention'.

τὸ πλεονεκτεῖν, καὶ τοῦτό ἐστιν τὸ ἀδικεῖν, τὸ πλέον τῶν ἄλλων ζητεῖν ἔχειν (483c3-5). The weaker segments of society, whom Callicles disdainfully calls φαυλότεροι (483c6), therefore are content to be on an equal footing with the stronger.

Callicles' belief in the survival of the fittest is firmly rooted. He argues that 'nature herself makes clear' that 'it is right for the superior to have more than the inferior and for the stronger to have more than the weaker' (483c8-d2).[9] Not only is he stating what he considers to be a fact but he is also advocating this state of affairs that 'nature herself' sanctions. 'Justice' (483d5: τὸ δίκαιον), as exhibited by nature, 'is judged' (κέκριται) to be the same for animals and for mankind. Callicles' conception of natural justice is expanded to include the assertion that it is right for the stronger to have sovereignty over the weaker (483d5); thus, "might is right."[10] His appeal to 'justice (according to nature)' is important because Callicles is unabashedly expressing the view that "might is right" is a just principle. Callicles, unlike Gorgias and Polus, has the courage to proclaim his beliefs, even if they are contrary to popular opinion.[11] By disregarding conventional notions of morality, he has set himself up as the spokesman for φύσις. Nature's definition of justice, not the definition supplied by νόμος (cf. 483c3-5 above), is valid for Callicles.

The bold reassertion of the credo that it is right for the stronger to have more than the weaker continues with Callicles' mention of Xerxes and his father Darius as examples of strong men who justified their invading the territory of others by virtue of nature's definition of justice (483e6-7: ἐπεὶ ποίῳ δικαίῳ χρώμενος Ξέρξης ἐπὶ τὴν Ἑλλάδα ἐστράτευσεν ἢ ὁ πατὴρ αὐτοῦ ἐπὶ Σκύθας;). The 'justification' or 'right' (τὸ δίκαιον)

---

9. Note that Callicles assumes that 'the better' are 'the stronger'.

10. It should be emphasized that Callicles endorses this state of affairs according to nature. Callicles is not merely stating what he sees, namely, that animals and humans everywhere are subject to the power of φύσις. He thinks that "the way things are (according to nature)" is "the way things should be."

11. Compare Callicles' courage to express openly his beliefs to Protagoras' claim that he alone admits to being a sophist and to have the ability to educate men (cf. *Protagoras* 317b3 and following).

employed by these two enemies of Greece is exactly the principle of nature that Callicles is advocating.¹² As his subversive speech continues, his words, though highly rhetorical, have a serious undertone. The juxtaposition of νόμος and φύσις in the phrase κατὰ νόμον γε τὸν τῆς φύσεως (483e3) is striking and paradoxical.¹³ Callicles unites νόμος and φύσις, which earlier were described as antithetical to one another (cf. 482e5-6), in a clever play upon words.¹⁴ He justifies the aggression of men like Xerxes, saying that their actions are 'in accordance with the nature of justice' (483e2: κατὰ φύσιν τὴν τοῦ δικαίου). This is followed by the emphatic assertion that there is a νόμος of nature that accounts for these actions.¹⁵ He is quick to point out that this νόμος is distinct from that established by man. In short, the actions of a Xerxes are justifiable in terms of nature's νόμος but not necessarily justifiable by man's. Callicles' self-conscious language here is important because he is using the words φύσις, τὸ δίκαιον and νόμος interchangeably; νόμος and φύσις, in the context of his argument, have now become fused and assimilated into his conception of 'justice' (τὸ δίκαιον). If one argues that the notions of 'law' (or 'convention'), 'nature', and 'justice' are related, as Callicles does, then the normative statement that it is right for the stronger to gain the advantage over the weaker can be viewed as a universal truth. Callicles strengthens his argument by appealing to "the law of nature" and thus makes the refutation of his views more difficult.

The Nietzschean overtones of Callicles' speech are most evident in his description of the enslavement of the strong by the

---

12. The boldness of Callicles' view is reinforced by his reference to the great enemies of Greece. He implies that Darius and Xerxes had a justification of their imperialism: φύσις.

13. Note the parallel phrases employed here: κατὰ φύσιν τὴν τοῦ δικαίου / κατὰ νόμον γε τὸν τῆς φύσεως (483e2-3). Callicles' wording implies that these phrases are somehow interchangeable, since they refer to a single (i.e., Callicles') conception of nature.

14. The expression νόμος τῆς φύσεως first appears here, although an allusion to this concept can be found in Thuc. 5.105.2.

15. The exclamation ναὶ μὰ Δία and the particle γε in 482e2-3 emphasize Callicles' insistence on the validity of his view regarding the contrast between the νόμος of nature and that laid down by man.

weak.[16] The best and strongest members of society are compared to 'lions'[17] (483e6: λέοντας): seized while still young, they are bewitched into slavery by the majority who say that 'equality is a necessary state of affairs' (484a1: τὸ ἴσον χρὴ ἔχειν).[18] Consequently, this state of 'equality' is defined as τὸ καλὸν καὶ τὸ δίκαιον (484a1-2) and is imposed by the weakest members of society as a means of restraining the strongest. Callicles, however, glorifies a different scenario where he envisions the existence of a man 'with sufficient natural strength' (φύσιν[19] ἱκανήν) who 'shakes off' (ἀποσεισάμενος) all of society's fetters and 'tramples on' (καταπατήσας) all 'learning, tricks, spells, and unnatural conventions' (γράμματα καὶ μαγγανεύματα καὶ ἐπῳδὰς καὶ νόμους παρὰ φύσιν[20]) (484a2-5). The description of the rise of the strong man uses imagery befitting an apotheosis;[21] the former slave now becomes society's 'master' (δεσπότης) and 'therein the justice of nature shines forth' (484a6-b1: ἐνταῦθα ἐξέλαμψεν τὸ τῆς φύσεως δίκαιον).

Note the consistent use of the gnomic aorist, which gives added weight to Callicles' description of the revolt of the *Übermensch*. He uses powerful words to characterize the violent reactions of the 'strong man' against his weaker oppressors. Also, the opposition between 'the justice of nature' and society's conception of justice is reasserted. The most striking statement (484a6-b1) is the one that precedes his Pindaric quotation. According to Callicles, the subjugation of

---

16. See Dodds 1959.387-391 for evidence that Nietzsche was influenced by the views attributed to Callicles by Plato.

17. The image of the lion here may have contributed to Nietzsche's depiction of *die blonde Bestie* in *Zur Genealogie der Moral* 1.11.

18. Note the sonorous quality of Callicles' words in 483e4-6. The onomatopoeic sound of Callicles' own lines mimics the bewitching effect of those spells and incantations which he says are used by the weak to enslave the strong. Compare *Meno* 80a2-3 for the collocation of the verbs γοητεύω ('beguile') and καταπᾴδω ('subdue by enchantment').

19. Like νόμος, φύσις can have various meanings in Callicles' speech.

20. I understand Callicles to imply that there are νόμοι which are 'natural' (κατὰ φύσιν).

21. True justice 'shines forth' (484b1: ἐξέλαμψεν) just as the former slave now 'reveals himself' (484a6: ἀνεφάνη) as master.

the weak by the strong is something to be exalted. His interpretation of 'justice according to nature' is not merely a statement of the workings of nature; it is an affirmation of the 'natural' state of affairs that sanctions the rule of the strongest over the weakest. In other words, I understand Callicles' position as follows: "It is only natural for the strong to have more than those who are weak; this is the way things are and this is the way they should be."

To support his point of view, Callicles quotes from a well-known poem of Pindar. Here is the Oxford text of the frequently discussed section of the *Gorgias* in which Callicles claims that Pindar expresses sentiments similar to his own:

δοκεῖ δέ μοι καὶ Πίνδαρος ἅπερ ἐγὼ λέγω ἐνδείκνυσθαι
ἐν τῷ ᾄσματι ἐν ᾧ λέγει ὅτι—
   νόμος ὁ πάντων βασιλεὺς
   θνατῶν τε καὶ ἀθανάτων·
οὗτος δὲ δή, φησίν, —
   ἄγει δικαιῶν τὸ βιαιότατον[22]
   ὑπερτάτᾳ χειρί· τεκμαίρομαι
   ἔργοισιν Ἡρακλέος, ἐπεί—ἀπριάτας—
λέγει οὕτω πως—τὸ γὰρ ᾆσμα οὐκ ἐπίσταμαι—λέγει δ' ὅτι οὔτε πριάμενος οὔτε δόντος τοῦ Γηρυόνου ἠλάσατο τὰς βοῦς, ὡς τούτου ὄντος τοῦ δικαίου φύσει, καὶ βοῦς καὶ τἆλλα κτήματα εἶναι πάντα τοῦ βελτίονός τε καὶ κρείττονος τὰ τῶν χειρόνων τε καὶ ἡττόνων.
(484b1-c3)

> And it seems to me that Pindar expresses what I am
> saying in that ode in which he writes—
>   *Nomos* is the sovereign of all,
>   Of mortals and immortals alike,
> and it is *nomos*, he says, that
>   Carries all, justifying the most violent deed
>   With victorious hand; this I prove

---

22. Although Burnet's *OCT* offers this reading of the text (i.e., Aristides' version), the best manuscripts (B, T, P, F) have βιαίων τὸ δικαιότατον.

> By the deeds of Herakles, for without paying
> the price—
> it runs something like that—for I do not know the poem by heart—but it says that he drove off the oxen of Geryon which were neither given to him nor paid for, because this is natural justice, that the cattle and all other possessions of the inferior and weaker belong to the superior and stronger.[23]

It is clear that Callicles assumes that his audience knows the Pindaric poem from which he is quoting. There is no doubt that this was a famous poem, since Herodotus, Pindar's contemporary, refers to it in the *Histories*. The context of Herodotus' reference to Pindar's gnome regarding νόμος as 'king of all' is the recounting of the contrast between the burial rites of the Greeks and the Indic Kallatiae (*Histories* 3.38). Herodotus is illustrating here his observation that every race prefers its own 'customs' (νόμοι) over those of others. Unlike the Greeks who burn the corpses of their fathers, the cannibalistic Kallatiae eat them. Both the Greeks and the Kallatiae expressed outrage at one another's respective practices. Herodotus then concludes with the remark: οὕτω μέν νυν ταῦτα νενόμισται, καὶ ὀρθῶς μοι δοκέει Πίνδαρος ποιῆσαι νόμον πάντων βασιλέα φήσας εἶναι (3.38).

Whether Herodotus' application of Pindar's gnome coincides with what the poet actually intended it to mean is not altogether certain. Martin Ostwald, for example, believes that Herodotus' interpretation of the Pindaric quote is correct, since νόμος, in its original context and in the Herodotean passage, refers to "a traditional attitude which implies certain deep-seated convictions and beliefs."[24] A different view is taken by Marcello Gigante who sees νόμος as meaning 'tradition, norm, custom' in Herodotus' application of the Pindaric phrase but Pindar himself meant something very different by νόμος. Pindar's meaning, Gigante argues, is not as "relativistic" as Herodotus';

---

23. Translation by W. D. Woodhead in Hamilton and Cairns (eds.) 1961.267; I have left *nomos* untranslated because of its wide range of meanings.

24. Ostwald 1965.124.

νόμος, in its Pindaric context, should be understood as "la legge che viene da Zeus, la legge divina universale che regge la storia del mondo."[25] Although I agree with Ostwald's definition of νόμος as used by Herodotus,[26] Gigante's contention that Herodotus' quotation of Pindar is tailored to suit the historian's own views, expressed within the context of this section of the *Histories*, is attractive. Socrates in the *Protagoras*, for example, can offer an interpretation of Simonides' poem that will promote his own system of beliefs in the face of Protagoras' sophistry. Like Protagoras, Herodotus quotes poetry out of context. He cites Pindar's gnome in order to defend his generalization regarding the attitude of men to their particular customs and rites. More importantly, even though Pindar's poem is fragmentary, one can ascertain from the other extant lines provided by *P. Oxy.* 2450 that the poet uses νόμος in a sense different from that of Herodotus.

Before one can comment upon Callicles' use of the Pindar quotation, one must determine the actual wording of Pindar and what he meant by the gnomic statement that νόμος is 'king of all'. Ever since Edgar Lobel first published the Oxyrhynchus papyrus in which the initial line seems to coincide with the last line of Callicles' quotation of fragment 169a and with his reference to Herakles' stealing of Geryon's cattle (*Gorgias* 484b11),[27] various scholars have offered differing interpretations of the fragmentary Pindaric poem as well as varied textual readings.[28] Scholars even disagree regarding its overall

---

25. Gigante 1956.111. Gigante's discussion of Herodotus' reference to Pindar (pp. 109-112) emphasizes the "parzialità dell' interpretazione erodotea" (109).

26. Cf. Ostwald 1965.124-125.

27. See Lobel 1961.141-154 for the *editio princeps* of the papyrus beginning from line 6 (ἐπεὶ Γηρυόνα βόας...).

28. A full bibliography of pre-1956 treatments can be found throughout Gigante's *ΝΟΜΟΣ ΒΑΣΙΛΕΥΣ* (1956). Some of the most helpful detailed discussions of fr. 169a are Ostwald 1965.109-138; Theiler 1965.69-80; Gigante 1966.286-311; Pavese 1968.47-88; and Lloyd-Jones 1972.45-56 (= 1990.154-165). The most recent text of fr. 169a in the 1989 Teubner edition of Pindaric fragments by H. Maehler is the one upon which I base my study.

metrical scheme.²⁹ Putting the controversial technical aspects of the fragment aside, one can nevertheless gain some insight into Pindar's treatment of the labors of Herakles, especially with regard to the hero's attacks on Geryon and Diomedes. The focus of my study of the Pindaric fragment is on the concept of νόμος, which, in my view, has its meaning altered by Callicles (or, more precisely, by Plato) in the context of his argument against Socrates. By Plato's time, the meaning of νόμος had become destabilized.

It is generally assumed that νόμος ὁ πάντων βασιλεύς is the first line of Pindar's poem.³⁰ Νόμος is 'king' of all things, both human and divine. Although some have compared this phrase to the Homeric formula describing Zeus, πατὴρ ἀνδρῶν τε θεῶν τε,³¹ the personification of νόμος as 'king' does not necessarily imply that Pindar is referring to Zeus or to Zeus' νόμος here. The personification of abstract concepts such as "time" or "love" is not uncommon in Greek poetry.³² Pindar's wording implies that Zeus himself, one of the immortals, is ruled by νόμος. It is interesting to note that the sophist Hippias in the *Protagoras*, presumably alluding to the same Pindaric poem cited by Callicles, describes νόμος as a 'tyrant of mankind' (337d2: τύραννος ὢν τῶν ἀνθρώπων). Hippias' negative portrayal of νόμος takes place in the context of his brief reference to the νόμος-φύσις antithesis, a favorite topic of the sophists. Pindar's use of the term, however, is free from any of its later connotations. Pindar regards νόμος as something powerful and inevitable; it holds sway over everything. The main verb of which νόμος is the subject, ἄγει (line 3), presents some difficulties. First, what is its translation? Pavese thinks that "the verb is used absolutely for leading by a divine agency"

---

29. Like Lobel and Lloyd-Jones, I think that the poem is probably a dithyramb.

30. Lloyd-Jones 1972.48 cites the beginning of the sixth Nemean ode (ἐν ἀνδρῶν, ἓν θεῶν γένος) as another example of Pindar's placing of a gnomic statement at the very start of a poem.

31. For example, Pavese 1968.55-57 and Lloyd-Jones 1972.48.

32. Pavese and Lloyd-Jones themselves provide examples of other personifications (e.g., Heraclitus' personification of πόλεμος as 'father and king of all' in Diels-Kranz 22 B 53).

and "this use of ἄγω corresponds to that of the epic ἡγέομαι."³³ However, merely to say that νόμος 'leads' causes the gnome's meaning to be too vague. Pindar has supplied us with an implied object from the surrounding context. Both Dodds and Ostwald think that the object of the verb is τὸ βιαιότατον. I agree with Lloyd-Jones (who cites *Nem.* 11.42-3: καὶ θνατὸν οὕτως ἔθνος ἄγει μοῖρα) that the object of ἄγει can be supplied from the immediately preceding θνατῶν τε καὶ ἀθανάτων and that τὸ βιαιότατον is the object of the participle δικαιῶν.³⁴ As 'king', νόμος presumably rules over 'all things, both human and divine'. Second, should one interpret θνατῶν τε καὶ ἀθανάτων in a narrow sense, referring to 'mortals and immortals' exclusively³⁵ and not to other entities?³⁶ This is an important question because its answer can lead to a better understanding of the meaning and prominence of νόμος in the fragment.

If it is assumed that δικαιῶν τὸ βιαιότατον is the correct text of the third line of fr. 169a,³⁷ problems of translation again arise. Pavese, like Lloyd-Jones, regards the verb δικαιῶν as factitive; however, the former translates it as 'bringing to justice' while the latter claims that the verb's form implies the meaning 'makes just'.³⁸ The meaning of this participle is uncertain

---

33. Pavese 1968.57. Dodds 1959.270 provides the tentative translation 'conducts (?)' for ἄγει; he later says that "488b3 suggests that Plato took ἄγει to mean 'plunders', as in the phrase ἄγειν καὶ φέρειν." Ostwald 1965.117 translates it as 'brings on'. All these translations seem inadequate.
34. Lloyd-Jones 1972.48.
35. Ibid.
36. Cf. *Isth.* 5.16 (θνατὰ θνατοῖσι πρέπει) for the adjective 'mortal' applied to things as well as human beings.
37. This is the reading found in the scholion on Pindar's *Nem.* 9.35a (quoting fr. 169a from νόμος down to χειρί) and Ael. Aristid. *or.* 45 (vol. 2, 68 Dindorf) and the corresponding scholion (vol. 3, 408 Dindorf). It also appears in the margin of V (Parisinus 2110), a Byzantine manuscript.
38. See the lengthy discussion by Pavese 1968.57-60. Lloyd-Jones 1972.49 rejects Pavese's interpretation, based on the fragmentary lines provided by the papyrus, that Herakles is bringing Diomedes' violent deeds to justice. Diomedes' motivation for resisting Herakles (line 15 of *P. Oxy.* 2450 refers to Diomedes' source of action: ἀρετᾷ) seems to support Lloyd-Jones' argument, which implies that Pindar does not blame Diomedes for

because δικαιόω is not found elsewhere in lyric poetry.[39] It is important to take note of the verb's rarity in lyric poetry because some have dismissed the variant reading βιαιῶν (βιαίων in mss. of the *Gorgias*) on the grounds that it is unattested. Although the Pindaric poem is fragmentary, one can say with little hesitation that δικαιῶν τὸ βιαιότατον suits the poem's context better than βιαιῶν τὸ δικαιότατον. Herakles' strength (βία) is a commonplace topic and it is therefore natural to assume that Pindar is referring to the *modus operandi* of Herakles, clearly a theme of the poem's subsequent lines regarding Geryon and Diomedes, by means of the abstract superlative τὸ βιαιότατον. It would be difficult to argue from the poem's extant contents that Pindar portrays Herakles' brutal ἔργα as examples or proofs of 'what is most just' (τὸ δικαιότατον).[40] Since he mentions Herakles' seizing Geryon's cattle without having paid for them (*Gorgias* 484b9: ἀπριάτας; cf. *P. Oxy.* 2450, line 8) and the hero's gruesome encounter with Diomedes' man-eating mares (lines 9ff. of the papyrus), the poet seems to have focused upon the violence of these "labors of Herakles."[41] It is impossible to determine the role of δίκη, if indeed it had any role at all, in Pindar's poem. If δικαιῶν τὸ βιαιότατον is accepted as the true Pindaric text, then the poet absolves Herakles from any wrongdoing because νόμος, by making δίκαιος that which is most violent, 'guides' (ἄγει) the affairs of gods and men.

The dative phrase ὑπερτάτᾳ χειρί also presents problems, since Aelius Aristides in his Περὶ ῥητορικῆς, evidently citing the Pindar fragment as quoted in the *Gorgias*, assumes that the

---

protecting his property. Like Lloyd-Jones, Dodds 1959.270 translates δικαιῶν as 'making just'.

39. See *LSJ* s. v. δικαιόω for an ambiguous translation ('to set right') of the verb in the context of fr. 169a alone.

40. Pindar cites some of Herakles' deeds as evidence (line 4: τεκμαίρομαι) in support of his gnome regarding νόμος. Perhaps Pindar regards Herakles' actions as not necessarily just in and by themselves but as part of the long-term process of justice (δίκη).

41. Note the phrase βίας ὁδόν (*P. Oxy.* 2450, line 19) as a possible reference to Herakles' labors.

'highest hand' belongs to Herakles and not to νόμος.⁴² Aelius Aristides, writing in the second century C.E. against Plato's views on oratory as expressed in the *Gorgias*, already demonstrates that this quote from Pindar had prompted possible misinterpretation throughout antiquity. Surely the 'supreme hand' (line 4) is that of νόμος (line 1); Aristides' paraphrase therefore is misleading, unless he infers that the 'hand' of νόμος is Herakles' by implication, since the hero's violent deeds are sanctioned by νόμος. Perhaps he confuses the reference to Herakles in the poem cited in the *Gorgias* with another taken from a different poem of Pindar. This is a plausible explanation of Aristides' error because he quotes from 'a certain dithyramb' of Pindar immediately after discussing the other passage cited by Callicles.⁴³ While explaining why Pindar refers to the deeds of Herakles in the quotation from the *Gorgias*, Aristides hypothesizes that the poet has another one of his works in mind. He quotes these lines from a Pindaric dithyramb: "Σὲ δ' ἐγὼ παρ' ἀμὶν" φησὶν, "αἰνέω μὲν Γηρυόνη, τὸ δὲ μὴ Διὶ φίλτερον σιγῷμι πάμπαν" (vol. 2, 70 Dindorf).⁴⁴ Pindar, whose poetry characteristically bestows praise (αἶνος) or blame (ψόγος), says in the lines cited by Aristides that he 'praises' (αἰνέω) Geryon in comparison to Herakles but he immediately interjects the phrase 'May I be altogether silent regarding that which is not pleasing (φίλτερον) to Zeus'.⁴⁵

Although I hesitate to claim that Pindar expresses the exact same sentiments toward Geryon in fr. 169a as he does in the dithyramb, I think that Aristides' quote from the dithyramb is instructive to the extent that here Pindar admits that Geryon is worthy of praise but the poet feels that Zeus would be

---

42. Ael. Arist. 45.53 (vol. 2, 70 Dindorf: εἰ γὰρ ἀξιώσει τὸ βιαιότατον νόμον εἶναι τὸν δικαιοῦντα καὶ τὴν ὑπερτάτην χεῖρα κρατεῖν Ἡρακλέους, ᾧ μετὰ τῆς χειρὸς τῶν δικαίων ἐμέλησεν, αὐτὴ [sc. ἡ ῥητορική] τοῖς ἑαυτῆς λόγοις ἀπολεῖται).

43. The dithyramb to which Aristides refers was entitled the *Cerberus* (cf. Wilamowitz 1922.344).

44. For the text of the Pindaric fragment cited by Aristides, see fr. 81 (dith. 2) Snell-Maehler.

45. Schol. Aristid. vol. 3, 409 Dindorf (σὲ δέ, ὦ Γηρυόνη, ἐπαινῶ παρ' αὐτὸν τὸν Ἡρακλέα...) makes it clear that the Pindaric text should be παρά μιν instead of παρ' ἀμίν.

displeased if Geryon were praised. In other words, there seems to be a dichotomy between Pindar's own sense of praiseworthy behavior and 'what is pleasing to Zeus'. The encomiastic poet defers to Zeus' authority over the matter even though he may think that Zeus' son, Herakles, behaves in an unjust fashion when he steals Geryon's cattle.[46] He quickly becomes silent for fear that Zeus may be offended by his opinion.[47] It is not unusual for Pindar to cut short his treatment of a subject that he thinks might be considered offensive.[48] 'Silence', says Pindar at one point, 'is often the wisest counsel for a man' (*Nem.* 5.18: καὶ τὸ σιγᾶν πολλάκις ἐστὶ σοφώτατον ἀνθρώπῳ νοῆσαι). However, just as Pindar implies in the dithyramb that Geryon is praiseworthy because he tries to resist Herakles' taking of the cattle by force (according to schol. Aristid. vol. 3, 409 Dindorf), a partial reconstruction of lines 15-17 of fr. 169a seems to indicate that Diomedes, like Geryon, is tacitly praised for having put up a struggle in defense of his property.[49] Diomedes acted out of ἀρετή, not out of κόρος (line 15: οὐ κό]ρῳ ἀλλ' ἀρετᾷ). In spite of the fragmentary state of the two Pindar poems, one

---

46. The scholiast explains that Pindar praises Geryon for defending his property when Herakles unjustly takes it away by force.

47. Crotty in 1982.105 aptly describes the situation: "The encomiast's role, then, is a circumscribed one. It is his duty to 'praise the praiseworthy, blame the blameworthy', and failure to do this is very wrong. The imperative is not absolute, however, because it depends ultimately on whether the gods are benevolent or hostile to the person, and the gods' disposition is not subject to men's notions of right and wrong. The power to exalt or humble—even without regard to a person's 'merits'—is a divine prerogative."

48. Cf. *Ol.* 13.91 and *Nem.* 5.17-18.

49. See Lloyd-Jones 1972.51 for a discussion of these lines. Unlike Pavese 1968.67ff., he thinks that Diomedes resisted Herakles' violence rather than vice versa. Pavese's view that Herakles resisted Diomedes contradicts what is said in the marginal scholion as restored and supplemented by Lobel in his 1961 publication of the papyrus fragment. Lobel's interpretation of the marginal scholion on the papyrus fragment, which he supplements by Ael. Aristid. vol. 2, 70 Dindorf and its corresponding scholion, is οὐκ ἐπὶ ὕβρει, ἀλλ' ἀρετῆς ἕνεκα. τὸ γὰρ [τὰ ἑαυτοῦ μὴ προ]ίεσθαι ἀνδρείου (ἐστίν) [ ] ἀλλ' οὐχ ὑβριστ[οῦ. Ἡρα]κλῆς δ(ὲ) ἠδί[ι]κει [ἀφελό]μενος.

can conclude with some certainty that Pindar treats the theme of the labors of Herakles in an ambivalent way. Herakles' foes, Geryon and Diomedes, are presented as worthy opponents who defend themselves against the violence of Zeus' son. Although Pindar thinks that it is right for these figures to try to resist Herakles' violent actions, he also simultaneously considers the violence of Herakles as something that can be justified. The justification inherent in Pindar's poems may be that Herakles' opponents are by nature monstrous and, consequently, unjust even though their reaction to Herakles is laudable. In addition, Herakles is the son of Zeus and his actions may be justifiable for this reason alone.

Pindar resorts to the concept of νόμος in order to justify or 'make just' that which is 'most violent' in both the human and divine spheres. I have hesitated to provide a translation or a definition of νόμος as used by Pindar in fr. 169a because I think that it has no direct English equivalent. Some understand Pindar to be referring to divine law. According to Hugh Lloyd-Jones, for example, "law for him was identical with the will of Zeus."[50] Marcello Gigante shares this opinion; however, he sees Orphic and Pythagorean overtones in Pindar's conception of νόμος.[51] However, Pindar's words explicitly state that νόμος is king of all, both mortal and immortal (fr. 169a, lines 1-2). Zeus himself, therefore, is subject to the power of νόμος.[52] Other scholars prefer to translate it as 'custom' or 'usage'. Martin Ostwald, for example, understands Pindar to mean "the common acceptance of a traditional belief as a valid and binding conviction"; the power of νόμος is "absolute, unchallengeable, and legitimate."[53] This definition is inadequate because it is

---

50. Lloyd-Jones 1972.56. Cf. Dodds 1959.270.

51. Cf. Gigante 1956.75. He is just one of many scholars who have postulated Orphic influences; see Ostwald 1965.120ff. for a lengthy discussion of the scholarly literature and a complicated argument against the interpretation of νόμος as 'divine law'.

52. Although Guthrie 1969.133 is right to point this out, his suggestion that νόμος be translated as 'recognized custom (usage, tradition)' does not clarify Pindar's meaning of the term in fr. 169a. Surely Pindar would not think that the violent acts of Herakles are somehow 'customary'; cf. Dodds 1959.270.

53. Ostwald 1965.125-126.

applicable only in the human sphere. The gods do not "accept" or "believe in" the power of νόμος; they are part of the process by which νόμος 'justifies that which is most violent'. Since this word can have the two different aforementioned meanings, it is possible that Pindar has a more general conception of what he means by νόμος than has been hitherto posited. Perhaps a fusion of the two prominent interpretations of the word would better capture the sense Pindar intends. Kevin Crotty's insightful remarks about the word's meaning may assist the search for a better translation:

> While *nomos* is divine therefore, it ought not to be severed from connotations of men's beliefs and values. *Nomos*, men's esteem or hatred for the heroes, is based not only on human notions of commendable behavior but also on the gods' love for or hostility towards the hero. *Nomos* refers to men's beliefs and evaluations, but Pindar is showing how these beliefs and evaluations are grounded in the gods' activity of exalting and humbling and may even contradict men's own notions of what is praiseworthy.[54]

This interpretation of the significance of νόμος in Pindar fr. 169a takes into account the inherent paradoxical nature of the term. The paradox arises out of its applicability to both gods and men. I agree with Crotty's view to the extent that I think that Pindar himself finds νόμος an ambiguous notion, since it refers to both 'divine law' and 'social usage'.[55] If a common denominator in the two proposed meanings of νόμος is sought, then another interpretation is possible.

The noun νόμος is thought to be etymologically related to the verb νέμω ('to allot'). Pindar could then be using νόμος in its basic sense as 'allotment' or 'apportionment'. I would suggest a somewhat more intricate definition of νόμος as suggested by the contents of fr. 169a; νόμος as 'king of all' is 'the way in which things are (apportioned)' or, in perhaps more general terms, 'the existing state of affairs'. This is an overarching

---

54. Crotty 1982.106.
55. Crotty 1982.104.

principle that is greater than gods and men.⁵⁶ Resembling a king who directs his kingdom, νόμος 'directs' (ἄγει) everything in its domain, namely, the universe. 'The way things are' is not a derivative concept; in other words, one cannot provide a rationale for it. Like Herakles, νόμος acts 'with arm supreme' (ὑπερτάτᾳ χειρί).⁵⁷ If I understand Pindar's intimations correctly, then the poet is claiming that one cannot understand why things happen the way they do, but he nevertheless believes that their final outcome is somehow just. Νόμος may then be viewed as the ultimate authority; it acts as if it were a just king. It empowers Herakles to bring 'utmost violence' (τὸ βιαιότατον) against Geryon and Diomedes, and although the hero's actions may be considered blameworthy by men, νόμος has "the power to overthrow normal human notions of right and wrong."⁵⁸ Herakles' violent encounters (fr. 169a) are 'justified' insofar as they are part of 'the existing state of affairs' understood by gods and men.

Callicles uses his quotation of Pindar in the *Gorgias* to defend the 'law of nature' as he interprets it. As has been suggested earlier, the concept of νόμος is a fluid one; by the fifth and fourth centuries, it has particular connotations that may not have attended Pindar's original meaning of the term in fr. 169a.⁵⁹ Callicles' view that it is always 'just, right' (δίκαιον) for the stronger to have the advantage over the weaker is his definition of νόμος, not Pindar's.⁶⁰ He cites the poet in order to support a position that seems far from what Pindar implies; Pindar tries to excuse Herakles' violent behavior by appealing to νόμος in order to justify it, whereas Callicles clearly expresses

---

56. The 'seventh' type of rule described by the Athenian at *Laws* 690c5-8 comes to mind as an example of the kind of power which Pindar's conception of νόμος possesses. The Athenian states that the rule which is 'dear to the gods and fortuitous' (θεοφιλῆ δέ γε καὶ εὐτυχῆ) is considered τὸ δικαιότατον by men. Men's adherence to the outcome of the casting of lots is an example of this type of ἀρχή.

57. I employ Lloyd-Jones' translation here (cf. p. 49).

58. Crotty 1982.105.

59. The νόμος-φύσις debate, in which νόμος is defined by human beings, is not relevant to Pindar's use of the term.

60. Cf. 483d1-e4 and note Callicles' phrase, κατὰ νόμον γε τὸν τῆς φύσεως, in particular.

the opinion that νόμος itself is the right of the stronger in all cases. It appears that Pindar's view of the term, which is more akin to 'the way things are', is reinterpreted by Callicles to signify 'the way things should be'. Callicles advocates 'nature's law'. Unlike Pindar, he actively supports the belief that it is right for the strong to be in a position of dominance. Therefore, one infers that Callicles does not think that behavior similar to Herakles' treatment of Geryon and Diomedes would need justification for the sheer reason that such treatment is 'right' (δίκαιον) in all cases; Herakles' forceful taking of Geryon's cattle is in accordance with 'the nature of justice' (484c1-3: ὡς τούτου ὄντος τοῦ δικαίου φύσει, καὶ βοῦς καὶ τἆλλα κτήματα εἶναι πάντα τοῦ βελτίονός τε καὶ κρείττονος τὰ τῶν χειρόνων τε καὶ ἡττόνων).[61] Pindar, on the other hand, seems to think it is necessary to make allowance for Herakles' use of violence.

The clearest display of Callicles' championing the right of the stronger is found in his exuberant generic description of the man of 'sufficient nature' (484a2: φύσιν ἱκανήν). 'Nature' (φύσιν) is used here as a synonym of 'strength'. Callicles' choice of words is noteworthy because it suggests that he is carefully selecting terms that make his argument cohesive; in his view, nature endorses the superiority of some men. Throughout his speech, Callicles focuses upon 'justice' (τὸ δίκαιον) as defined by nature.[62] The man of 'sufficient nature' disregards unnatural laws and conventions; Callicles implies that these are man-made and imposed by weaker men upon the stronger. Therefore, they are not 'natural' because they curb the stronger man's right to claim more than the weaker does. It is important to note Callicles' emphasis on the stronger's "rightful" claim, which can be described as τὸ δίκαιον, because Socrates' interlocutor is claiming that nature's favoring the stronger, a νόμος φύσεως, is to be defended on the grounds that 'natural justice' is preferable to justice as defined by men. Callicles' sequence of

---

61. Callicles' diction here is noteworthy because he assumes that 'the stronger man' (ὁ κρείττων) is automatically 'the better man' (ὁ βελτίων) and he thus implies that nature's definition of justice has a sound moral backing.

62. Cf. 483d1-e2 and 484a1-b1.

thought implies that it is not only natural for the stronger to have more than the weaker; unlike 'having an equal share' (484a1: τὸ ἴσον ἔχειν), which is society's definition of τὸ καλὸν καὶ τὸ δίκαιον (484a1-2), the νόμος φύσεως defended by Callicles is that which is 'good and just'.

When Callicles cites Pindar, his purpose is to show that his view of natural justice is not novel. Like Socrates who interprets Simonides' poem in the *Protagoras*, Callicles transforms the meaning of Pindar's poem to suit the particular philosophical stance that he himself is espousing in the *Gorgias*; specifically, the right of the stronger. Since he has shifted Pindar's original meaning of the gnomic statement νόμος ὁ πάντων βασιλεύς..., so that νόμος in the fragment is now interpreted as signifying the 'law of nature' (as described in 483e and following), it is conceivable that Plato can have Callicles alter the original text of the quotation in order to defend his vehement standpoint. A purposeful misquotation of Pindar's words on the part of Plato, attributed to Callicles, would not only characterize Socrates' interlocutor as one of those men who dare to 'trample upon' society's γράμματα (cf. 484a4) but it would also serve to reinforce Callicles' own view that νόμος, interpreted as the right of the stronger to have more than the weaker, is itself καλὸς καὶ δίκαιος and that violent behavior on the part of the stronger in order to rule and have more than the weaker is 'right' according to 'the law of nature'. In other words, if Callicles were to misquote Pindar, Plato would be painting a clearer picture of Callicles' personality instead of merely having Callicles cite Pindar as an authoritative source in defense of Callicles' views. If one believes that Plato is capable of purposeful misquotation for the sake of an insightful and ironical glimpse into his portrayal of Callicles' character, then it is plausible that the variant reading βιαίων[63] τὸ δικαιότατον found within the manuscripts is not necessarily the result of a scribal error involving spoonerism.[64] Although most editors of the *Gorgias* emend the text so that it accords with Pindar's δικαιῶν τὸ

---

63. The correct accentuation would be βιαιῶν.

64. Dodds 1959.272 argues that the manuscript reading is this type of textual corruption; cf. Ostwald 1965.132 n. 8, Pavese 1968.57 n. 22, and Crotty 1982.155 n. 1.

βιαιότατον, cited in schol. *Nem.* 9.35a and Ael. Arist. *or.* 45 (vol. 2, 68 Dindorf),[65] some scholars accept the reading found in the manuscripts as the original Platonic text.[66] In spite of the majority opinion, which argues against the possibility of Plato's purposely having Callicles misquote Pindar, I think that both sides of the issue should be studied, especially in light of the quotation's context within the dialogue. This necessitates a brief look at the complicated argumentation employed by the two opposing viewpoints.

The argument most often used against the reading provided by the manuscript tradition is that the verb βιαιόω is unattested; consequently, its meaning is unclear. Βιάζω (or the deponent βιάζομαι) is the attested verb related to the substantive βία. What would βιαιῶν, if its existence as a verb in Greek is allowed, mean in relation to its object, τὸ δικαιότατον?[67] Wilamowitz, who believes that the corrupt reading βιαιῶν stems from Plato's accidental misquotation of Pindar caused by a lapse of memory (*ein Gedächtnisfehler*), thinks that its meaning would correspond to that of βιαζόμενος.[68] According to his account, the Pindaric phrase as misquoted here by Plato is understood by Libanius, who supposedly paraphrases the Pindaric lines as found in his text of Plato, to mean 'violating justice'.[69]

---

65. Cf. the *OCT* edition of Plato's dialogues by Burnet (vol. 3) and Dodds's edition of the *Gorgias* (p. 123).

66. E.g., É. Des Places 1949.171ff., J. Irigoin 1952.16-17, Taylor 1960.117 n. 2, Friedländer 1964(2).260-61, and Grote 1994.21-31. For a detailed discussion of the manuscript tradition for the *Gorgias*, see Dodds 1959.34-56.

67. The false accent found in the manuscripts (βιαίων) can be explained as a copyist's error. Perhaps the error is somehow "learned," since βιαίων is the genitive plural of the adjective βίαιος and is found in legal terminology (e.g., δίκη βιαίων) employed by orators such as Lysias and Demosthenes (cf. *LSJ s. v.* βίαιος).

68. Cf. Wilamowitz 1920(2).97.

69. Wilamowitz (pp. 98-99) regards βιάζεται τὸ δίκαιον in Libanius *Apol. Socr.* 87 as a paraphrase of βιαιῶν τὸ δικαιότατον. Lloyd-Jones 1972.48 also believes that Libanius adopts the text of the Pindaric lines from a manuscript of Plato.

Wilamowitz sees another instance of this same accidental misquotation of Pindar's poem in the *Laws* (890a4-5: εἶναι τὸ δικαιότατον ὅτι τις ἂν νικᾷ βιαζόμενος).[70] It is uncertain that Plato has the Pindar quotation in mind here, and the reference in *Laws* 690b7-c3 to the natural 'rule' (690c3: ἀρχή) of the wise over the ignorant, in which Wilamowitz sees another accidental misquotation of the same Pindaric lines by Plato, is not necessarily an allusion to the gnome quoted by Callicles in the *Gorgias*, even if the Athenian speaker mentions Pindar by name in this passage.[71] An explicit Platonic reference to Pindar's poem in *Laws* 715a1-2 (καὶ ἔφαμέν που κατὰ φύσιν τὸν Πίνδαρον ἄγειν δικαιοῦντα τὸ βιαιότατον, ὡς φάναι) forces Wilamowitz to conjecture that the "correct" text of Pindar later found its way into the manuscript tradition, thus replacing Plato's original misquotation here.[72]

The problems caused by the argumentation of Wilamowitz are numerous, however. First, he cannot adequately account for the "correct" allusion to Pindar's poem in *Laws* 715a and for the Pindaric text as quoted by Aristides who, since he is defending rhetoric against Plato's criticism in the *Gorgias*, presumably quotes from a manuscript of the dialogue that has the reading δικαιῶν τὸ βιαιότατον by the second century C.E., two centuries earlier than that of Libanius who supposedly is paraphrasing the Platonic misquotation βιαιῶν τὸ δικαιότατον in his Ἀπολογία Σωκράτους. If one follows Wilamowitz, then

---

70. Although Dodds 1959.271 argues "there is nothing to prove that Plato had the Pindar passage in mind here," the claim of Wilamowitz that this passage in the *Laws* alludes to Pindar's poem may have been prompted by the words immediately preceding the alleged reference; the Athenian speaker attributes the attitude expressed in the supposed paraphrase to poets as well as to other ἄνδρες σοφοί (cf. 890a4).

71. The Athenian's reference to Pindar deals with the poet's opinion regarding the rule of the wise. Consequently, he may be alluding to a nonextant poem of Pindar. The opinion expressed in *Laws* 690c1-3 seems to counter one which is attributed to Pindar: καίτοι τοῦτό γε, ὦ Πίνδαρε σοφώτατε, σχεδὸν οὐκ ἂν παρὰ φύσιν ἔγωγε φαίην γίγνεσθαι, κατὰ φύσιν δέ, τὴν τοῦ νόμου ἑκόντων ἀρχὴν ἀλλ' οὐ βίαιον πεφυκυῖαν. In addition, the Athenian mentions the 'rule of the stronger' immediately before turning to the words of Pindar in 690b7-8 as support for his view.

72. Wilamowitz 1920(2).98.

it is difficult to explain why Aristides offers the "genuine" Pindaric reading, which one assumes that he obtains from a manuscript of Plato, while Libanius, who one presumes is using a manuscript of Plato two centuries later, paraphrases the alternate reading or "misquotation." The chronology of these two references to the Pindar quotation implies that textual corruption may have occurred between the time of Aristides and that of Libanius. An alternative hypothesis involves postulating the existence of competing manuscript traditions of Plato during antiquity, one containing the "genuine" Pindaric reading and the other the "misquotation."

A second possible explanation involves the presence of an alternative reading (either a learned copyist's correction [δικαιῶν τὸ βιαιότατον] of a Platonic misquotation or a possible corruption resulting from spoonerism [βιαιῶν τὸ δικαιότατον]) in the margin of a Plato manuscript, which later intruded into the text and ultimately replaced the genuine Platonic reading. What is certain, however, is that Libanius had access to the two readings because he creates an imaginary scenario in which Socrates is defending himself against Anytus who, according to Libanius, purposely altered Pindaric poetry in order to attack Socrates:

οὕτω καὶ περὶ Πινδάρου διαλέγεται δεδοικὼς αὐτοῦ τὴν διδαχὴν καὶ φοβούμενος μή τις τῶν νέων ἀκούσας ὡς ὑπερτάτῃ χειρὶ βιάζεται τὸ δίκαιον ἀμελήσας τῶν νόμων ἀσκῇ τὼ χεῖρε. καὶ τοῦτο οὕτως εἰκότως ὑφορᾶται Σωκράτης, ὡς ὁ σοφώτατος Ἄνυτος ἐτόλμησε μεταγράψαι τὸ τοῦ ποιητοῦ καθάπερ ἐν Σκύθαις διαλεγομένου καὶ οὐκ εἰσομένοις ἀνθρώποις, τί μὲν Ἀνύτου, τί δὲ Πινδάρου. ἀλλὰ τοῦτο μὲν καλῶς ἐποίησε κακουργῶν. ἐν γὰρ τῷ μεταθεῖναι τὸ τοῦ ποιητοῦ κατηγόρηκε τοῦ Πινδάρου καὶ τὸν Σωκράτην ἐπῄνεσεν.

(*Apol. Socr.* 87 Foerster)

Thus he [Anytus] also discusses Pindar in fear of the poet's teaching, lest some youth, upon hearing that "justice is violated by a supreme hand," would exercise his own hands in disregard of the law. Socrates naturally found this suspect, since the very clever Anytus dared to

alter the poet's words as if Pindar were talking among
Scythians and not among those who would know which
words belonged to Pindar and which to Anytus. But a
good thing resulted from his misdeed, for in changing the
poet's verse he attacked Pindar and praised Socrates.

This difficult passage from Libanius' *Apology*, which presents a fictitious account of the trial of Socrates, says that Anytus brought up the subject of Pindar (περὶ Πινδάρου διαλέγεται) in his accusation against Socrates. Libanius has Anytus fear Pindar's teaching (διδαχήν), supposedly spread by Socrates, which would inspire young men to 'violate justice' and disregard established laws. However, Anytus fails in his indictment of Socrates because he 'dared to alter Pindar's words' (ἐτόλμησε μεταγράψαι τὸ τοῦ ποιητοῦ). Socrates 'sees beneath' (ὑφορᾶται) Anytus' ploy. By changing Pindar's meaning, Anytus manages unwittingly to help Socrates' cause and to speak against Pindar.

The problem presented by this passage is the paraphrase of Pindar's 'teaching': ὑπερτάτῃ χειρὶ βιάζεται τὸ δίκαιον. Libanius does not indicate whence he derives this episode involving Anytus' purposeful misquotation of Pindar employed as an indictment against Socrates. An immense amount of scholarly conjecture regarding Libanius' sources has resulted in the assumption that material from the lost Κατηγορία Σωκράτους of Polycrates, itself a fictitious account of Socrates' prosecution written sometime around the first quarter of the fourth century B.C.E., is used by Libanius.[73] However, Libanius never refers to Polycrates or his work even though he mentions the name of Xenophon whose *Apology* he definitely uses as a source.[74] Since Libanius has Anytus refer to the same Pindaric lines as does Callicles, scholars have extrapolated that there must be some type of relationship between the *Gorgias* and the lost work of Polycrates (assumed to be Libanius' source). One must bear in mind, however, that Polycrates is not necessarily Libanius'

---

73. For a detailed discussion of the scholarly literature on this topic, see Markowski 1910.20-66. Cf. Foerster 1909.1-4 and Dodds's comments in 1959.28-29, 271-72.

74. I am grateful to Albert Henrichs for bringing this to my attention.

source for the reference to Anytus' citation of Pindar, and the fact that Callicles and Anytus refer to the same well-known Pindar poem does not imply, as Wilamowitz maintains in his clever attempt to date the *Gorgias*, that the dialogue is Plato's response to Polycrates' work.[75] Like Taylor, I think that it is unlikely that Polycrates "could have used a misquotation put by Plato into the mouth of Callicles to damage the reputation of Socrates."[76]

Since it is impossible to determine whether or not there was a relationship between the *Gorgias* and Polycrates' lost pamphlet, it seems fruitless to argue (as does Wilamowitz) that Polycrates had corrected Plato's unintentional misquotation and that Anytus later charged Polycrates with altering Plato's text.[77] It is unnecessary to postulate such a complicated explanation for Libanius' having access to the two different versions of Callicles' quotation of Pindar. Libanius could have been using a manuscript of Plato that contained βιαιῶν τὸ δικαιότατον while simultaneously reading Aristides' speech in defense of oratory that had the genuine "Pindaric" text.[78] Perhaps it was Libanius who, when confronted with the variant readings in Plato and Aristides, contrived the imaginary scene in which Anytus misquotes, just as another of Socrates' opponents, namely, Callicles, appears to have done.

Although many scholars favor the alternative explanation for the variant readings—that textual corruption in the form of a

---

75. Wilamowitz 1920(2).99ff. Most scholars (e.g., Markowski, Foerster, Dodds, and Wilamowitz) accept Libanius' use of Polycrates as a given, even though it can be argued that Libanius obtains much of the material for his fictitious work from the dialogues of Plato and Xenophon's *Apology*. In addition, it is possible that Libanius himself creates the situation of Anytus' purposeful misquotation of Pindar. I would like to think that Libanius, using a Plato manuscript with a variant reading of Pindar as quoted by Callicles and juxtaposing it with the Pindar text as found in Aelius Aristides, is responsible for attributing the act of purposeful misquotation to Anytus who, like Callicles, is an opponent of Socrates. Even if my conjecture is wrong, I do not think that one can be certain of the influence of Polycrates' pamphlet on the contents of the Libanius passage.

76. Taylor 1960.104 (cf. Dodds 1959.271).
77. Cf. Wilamowitz 1920(2).99.
78. See Pack 1947.17-20 for Aristides' influence on Libanius.

"spoonerism" must have occurred between the time of Aristides and that of Libanius[79]—their argument disregards Callicles' words at 484b10 where he explicitly states that he does not know what Pindar's poem exactly says: λέγει οὕτω πως—τὸ γὰρ ᾆσμα οὐκ ἐπίσταμαι. This comment would appear superfluous if Callicles had not misquoted a famous Pindaric passage. The suggestion that Plato intentionally has Callicles misquote should be considered in light of the added irony of Callicles' misquotation. While βιαιῶν τὸ δικαιότατον could mean 'violating that which is most just', Callicles' words would have more effect if he quotes Pindar as describing the power of νόμος by the phrase 'enforcing (i.e., effecting by force) that which is most just'.[80] Interpreting βιαιῶν in the latter sense would be more appropriate with respect to the immediate context of Callicles' quotation. Immediately before his reference to Pindar's poem, Callicles takes pains to demonstrate that the νόμος of nature, which sanctions the advantage of the strong over the weak, establishes a state of affairs that is in itself right and just. In other words, τὸ δικαιότατον could refer to the ideal scene described in 483e-484a. *Theognidea* 255 reads κάλλιστον τὸ δικαιότατον and, by extension, it could be claimed that Callicles has described what is κάλλιστον in his eyes: the rebellion of the powerful against the constraints of society. If one allows for the possibility that Callicles misquotes Pindar, then his incorrect citing of the poet's words about νόμος is used as a feeble support for his own viewpoint. In addition, it would seem quite comical if Plato not only presented Callicles' perverse view but also had Callicles attribute such an opinion to Pindar.

---

79. See n. 64 above.
80. Those who believe that Plato puts a misquotation in Callicles' mouth translate, for the most part, βιαιῶν as 'violating'; cf. Des Places 1949.173 and Irigoin 1952.17. Callicles would be undermining his own position if he were to say that νόμος 'violates' justice. Charles Segal has suggested to me that βιαιόω may be a factitive verb like δικαιόω; therefore, the phrase βιαιῶν τὸ δικαιότατον would mean 'making τὸ δικαιότατον into βία'.

# 4

# STESICHORUS' PALINODE
# IN THE *PHAEDRUS**

Socrates' reference to Stesichorus' famous palinode in the *Phaedrus* has not been studied with respect to its context. Although scholars have focused upon the palinode with respect to the question of whether or not Stesichorus composed more than one "recantation," few have analyzed its role within the dialogue.[1] It is curious that Plato has Socrates present a lengthy speech in order to retract it. Why does Socrates fabricate an elaborate oration in support of a view that he later critiques? More importantly, why does Socrates incorporate the palinode of Stesichorus into the framework of his disquisition on erotic love? Plato may, of course, be merely drawing a comparison between Socrates' supposed reversal of opinion concerning the nature of ἔρως and Stesichorus' retraction of his former denigrating portrayal of Helen. Nevertheless, it is worth considering whether Plato has Socrates adopt the *persona* of the lyric poet Stesichorus, and suggesting that Socrates' view of himself as one who is μουσικός characterizes the nature of his own sub-

---

* Reprinted by permission of the publisher from *Classical World* (90.4) copyright © 1997.

1. See Sider 1989.423 for an extensive bibliography on the various interpretations of the ancient testimonia regarding the palinode(s) of Stesichorus. De Martino 1979.255-260 provides one of the only discussions of Socrates' "imitation" of Stesichorus' palinode. He argues (pp. 258-59) that although Stesichorus composed two palinodes, the structure of the *Phaedrus* requires Socrates to offer a single palinode because Socrates' first speech should be considered in conjunction with the speech of the absent Lysias (read by Phaedrus). Some recent philosophical interpretations of the *Phaedrus* are Nussbaum 1986.200-233, Ferrari 1987, and Rossetti (ed.) 1992.

sequent "palinode." Although Socrates, like Stesichorus, composes his own "palinode" in order to avert potential divine retribution, his comments to the young Phaedrus regarding love and poetry as types of divine inspiration reflect his own poetic inspiration in the dialogue. The purpose of this study is to argue that Plato portrays Socrates in the *Phaedrus* as an inspired poet and lover who, unlike Lysias, can teach Phaedrus about the true nature of love by way of philosophy rather than through the medium of rhetoric.

While censuring Homer for his failure to correct his mistakes, Socrates praises Stesichorus for employing a καθαρμός ('purification'), in the form of the palinode, to correct his earlier mistake.[2] Socrates' diction is colored by these notions of ritual purification and lyric sensibilities. One infers that Socrates, unlike the epic poet Homer but like the lyric poet Stesichorus, is μουσικός ('one who has a true relationship with the Muses').[3] It is significant that Socrates praises a *lyric* poet. Perhaps Plato is indirectly lauding lyric poetry by way of comparing Socrates to a poet like Stesichorus who, by "setting the record straight" concerning the glorious deeds of earlier times, is communicating to the *polis* positive moral values. Socrates has an objective similar to Stesichorus'. He is trying to impart to the young Phaedrus an ennobling comprehension of the nature of love rather than aiming at a mere refutation of the sophistic speech of Lysias. Like Stesichorus, Socrates is being

---

2. One infers that Homer is depicted as ignorant of the use of the palinode as a means of curing the blindness which he incurred by offending the gods in the process of storytelling (243a3-4). There is a possibility that Homer, in addition to Stesichorus, is portrayed here as being guilty of blasphemy against Helen in particular.

3. Socrates attributes Stesichorus' understanding of the cause of his own blindness to his being μουσικός (*Phaedrus* 243a5-7). Although this adjective may designate a *lyric* poet, another of its connotations is clear in the immediate context. Socrates emphasizes Stesichorus' relationship with the Muses. Plato portrays Socrates throughout his "palinode" to Eros as someone else who, although not a poet, has this special relationship with the Muses (cf. 248d3 where Socrates attributes the quality of being μουσικός, along with other characteristics, to the superior soul of the philosopher).

portrayed by Plato as an educator who corrects misguided thought.

More importantly, Plato contrasts the two very different types of "lovers' education" espoused by Lysias and Socrates respectively. Both figures can be viewed as potential ἐρασταί ('lovers') of Phaedrus who offer the youth (ὁ παῖς) their individual arguments for the sake of winning the youth's love and admiration. What I mean by the phrase "lovers' education" is the notion that love and education (παιδεία) are interrelated in the eyes of the Greeks, and this conceptual framework is the basis of Socrates' views on the nature of love as portrayed in the *Phaedrus*.[4] Socrates attempts to persuade Phaedrus that a relationship of love between two individuals entails the mutual education of their souls. Consequently, Socrates' speech to Phaedrus should be regarded as a reflection of his love for the young man. Philosophical discourse, practiced by Socrates in his dialogue with Phaedrus, tries to displace sophistic oratory, employed by Lysias, as a means of communication between lovers. It is only a philosopher who can be a lover of beauty, a lover of the Muses, and a lover. Plato has Socrates fulfill all of these functions in the course of the dialogue.

Socrates' quotation of Stesichorus occurs after his own speech that supposedly is meant to counter Lysias' λόγος. Phaedrus has just read aloud, at Socrates' behest, Lysias' speech in which the orator maintains that 'one ought to bestow favor upon a nonlover rather than upon a lover' (cf. 227c7-8: λέγει γὰρ ὡς χαριστέον μὴ ἐρῶντι μᾶλλον ἢ ἐρῶντι). Socrates, unlike the young Phaedrus, is unimpressed by Lysias' speech.[5] He says that he would be challenged by the 'wise men and women of old' if he were to agree with Phaedrus' high opinion of Lysias' rhetorical display. Socrates here (235b7-9), as in the *Protagoras*, for example (cf. 345e), feels that the orators are upstarts in comparison to the παλαιοὶ καὶ σοφοὶ ἄνδρες ('wise men and women of old'). Although he cannot remember offhand in what context he has heard a better account

---

4. See Lewis 1985.197-222 for a discussion of the relationship between παιδεία ('education') and παιδεραστία ('love of boys') as exemplified in the Theognidean corpus.

5. Note that Socrates calls Lysias a 'poet' at 234e6.

than Lysias' treatment of love, he asserts that the works of lyric poets such as Sappho and Anacreon and of some prose writers are doubtless better than Lysias' λόγος regarding love (235c2-4: δῆλον δὲ ὅτι τινῶν ἀκήκοα, ἤ που Σαπφοῦς τῆς καλῆς ἤ Ἀνακρέοντος τοῦ σοφοῦ ἤ καὶ συγγραφέων τινῶν).[6] Socrates' opinion that Sappho and Anacreon are better authorities than Lysias on erotic matters does not seem ironic in the immediate context because Socrates continues to claim that he himself could speak better than Lysias regarding love. It is important to notice Socrates' words here because he is describing himself as though he were a seer or a poet who is inspired by an external source:

> ὅτι μὲν οὖν παρά γε ἐμαυτοῦ οὐδὲν αὐτῶν ἐννενόηκα, εὖ οἶδα, συνειδὼς ἐμαυτῷ ἀμαθίαν· λείπεται δὴ οἶμαι ἐξ ἀλλοτρίων ποθὲν ναμάτων διὰ τῆς ἀκοῆς πεπληρῶσθαί με δίκην ἀγγείου.
>
> (235c6-d1)
>
> I am of course well aware it can't be anything originating in my own mind, for I know my own ignorance; so I suppose it can only be that it has been poured into me, through my ears, as into a vessel.[7]

In spite of his usual claim that he is conscious of his ignorance, Socrates is setting the stage for his subsequent discussion of love, which is, in addition to prophecy and poetry, a type of divine 'madness' (μανία). The 'external streams' that fill the ears of Socrates, who likens himself to a 'vessel' (ἀγγεῖον), do not necessarily derive from the wise men and women of an older generation. Socrates, while educating the young Phaedrus

---

6. De Vries 1969.74 provides a thorough discussion of Socrates' reference to the poets here, especially with regard to the meaning of the adjectives καλῆς and σοφοῦ as applied to Sappho and Anacreon respectively. Cf. 258a6 for another instance of the term συγγραφεύς designating 'prose-writer'. Fortenbaugh 1966.108-109 argues that Socrates' subsequent speeches contain allusions to the poems of Sappho and Anacreon.

7. English translations of passages from the *Phaedrus* are by R. Hackforth in Hamilton and Cairns (eds.) 1961.476-525, with the permission of Cambridge University Press.

regarding the best and most divine madness of all—love—is portrayed as one who is himself divinely inspired not only by Eros during his "palinode" to the deity but also by the Muses and the 'god-inhabited' pastoral setting in which their conversation takes place.⁸

Since the focus of this study is Socrates' quotation of Stesichorus' palinode, it is necessary to look briefly at Socrates' first speech, which he later recants in his own palinode that is designed to avert the wrath of the god of love. Socrates, who describes himself as 'a lover of speeches' (ἀνὴρ φιλόλογος),⁹ pretends that Phaedrus has compelled him to deliver a speech designed to outdo Lysias' (cf. 236b2 and 236e4-5). Before he offers his oration, he says that he will cover his head, run through the speech as quickly as possible, and not look at Phaedrus, since he would feel shame if he were to run into trouble (or 'be at a loss') at some point: ἐγκαλυψάμενος ἐρῶ, ἵν' ὅτι τάχιστα διαδράμω τὸν λόγον καὶ μὴ βλέπων πρὸς σὲ ὑπ' αἰσχύνης διαπορῶμαι (237a4-5). This statement is a foreshadowing of Socrates' subsequent repudiation of the views he is about to express in this first speech. It is odd that Socrates would cover his head and hurry through a disquisition in which he has the opportunity to counter Lysias' rhetoric. I interpret Socrates' gestures as purposeful hinting on Plato's part; Socrates covers his head, since he is already ashamed of what he is about to do.¹⁰

---

8. Cf. Socrates' words at 238c9-d1: τῷ ὄντι γὰρ θεῖος ἔοικεν ὁ τόπος εἶναι. He provides a brief description of the locale at 230b2-c5. The dialogue ends with Socrates' prayer to Pan and the other deities of this seemingly sacred place (279b8-c3). For the role of this prayer in the dialogue as a whole, see Rosenmeyer 1962.34-44, Clay 1979.345-353, Griswold 1986.226-229, Gaiser 1989.105-140, and Motte in Rossetti (ed.) 1992.320-23. See also the insightful discussion of the importance of the dialogue's setting by H. Görgemanns in Most, Petersmann, and Ritter (eds.) 1993.122-147.

9. The word φιλόλογος, in the context of 236e5, probably means 'a lover of speeches', although it may also refer to Socrates' fondness for discourse.

10. Cf. 242c8 for Socrates' subsequent claim that he felt troubled and fearful while he had delivered his first speech: ἐμὲ γὰρ ἔθραξε μέν τι καὶ πάλαι λέγοντα τὸν λόγον, καί πως ἐδυσωπούμην.... Perhaps Socrates is

Socrates could never deliver wholeheartedly a speech that would agree with Lysias' pragmatic views on love. Socrates, to accommodate the young and impressionable Phaedrus, agrees to give a better speech containing the same overall gist as Lysias'; however, he will 'run through the speech as quickly as possible', since it will not truly reflect his own opinion. Moreover, he dares not to look at Phaedrus not only because he is ashamed to appear as a worse ποιητής (as compared to Lysias) in the eyes of the youth but also because he is ashamed of the view he is about to expound. Socrates, whose role as Phaedrus' older potential suitor and educator is intimated by Plato throughout the dialogue, feels shame, since he will be teaching a young ἐρώ-μενος ('beloved') to have an impious view regarding Eros. Socrates' symbolic gesture is, as one discovers later in the dialogue, related to his quotation of Stesichorus' palinode. The legend that Stesichorus lost his sight because of his defamation of Helen is analogous to Socrates' lack of vision during the speech he delivers with his head covered. Socrates' blindness is metaphorical as well as real when he first discusses love because what he says while his head is covered he later retracts by way of a 'true account' or, in Stesichorus' terms, an ἔτυμος λόγος (243a8), which is his own palinode to Eros. Immediately before delivering his palinode, which is intended as an apotropaic gesture, Socrates uncovers his head. When in reality he regains his vision (at 243b6-7), he simultaneously regains his figurative sight into the true nature of love.

Socrates invokes the Muses for inspiration (237a7-9) before embarking upon his first monologue.[11] Already he has begun to assume the guise of a poet. Socrates, after a lengthy preamble, defines love as some kind of desire (ἐπιθυμία: 238b8; cf. 237d2). He then interrupts his speech, asking Phaedrus whether he agrees with the view that Socrates has undergone a religious experience (238c6: θεῖον πάθος πεπονθέναι). Socrates is referring to his divine inspiration, which is derived from the

---

reenacting here a performative gesture indicating blindness, a gesture which Stesichorus allegedly employed while delivering his palinode to Helen; cf. Sider 1989.430.

11. Note Socrates' "epic" diction here, especially his use of the epithet λίγειαι ('clear-voiced') modifying the Muses.

'divine' (θεῖος) locality. He likens his state to 'possession by Nymphs':

> τῷ ὄντι γὰρ θεῖος ἔοικεν ὁ τόπος εἶναι, ὥστε ἐὰν ἄρα πολλάκις νυμφόληπτος προϊόντος τοῦ λόγου γένωμαι, μὴ θαυμάσῃς· τὰ νῦν γὰρ οὐκέτι πόρρω διθυράμβων φθέγγομαι.
>
> (238c9-d3)

For truly there seems to be a divine presence in this spot, so that you must not be surprised if, as my speech proceeds, I become as one possessed; already my style is not far from dithyrambic.

Socrates' statement foreshadows the theme of 'possession' or 'madness' (μανία) that is used in his future description of the state of being in love. More importantly, he is describing his divine inspiration in terms of 'possession'; he thinks his madness may be attributed to the Nymphs of the locale.[12] His attributing the source of his madness to the Nymphs reappears at 241e3-5 when he hesitates to continue the tenor of this speech. Surely Phaedrus knows that Socrates will be possessed by the Nymphs into whose clutches the young man deliberately has thrown him (ἆρ' οἶσθ' ὅτι ὑπὸ τῶν Νυμφῶν, αἷς με σὺ προύβαλες ἐκ προνοίας, σαφῶς ἐνθουσιάσω;).[13] Socrates' description of his present utterance as 'not far from dithyrambic' (238d2-3) is probably ironic insofar as the most famous composers of the dithyramb were already dead by the fourth century.[14] However, one must bear in mind that Socrates considers

---

12. For a discussion of the Greek views regarding nympholepsy, see Connor 1988.155-189. Note in particular Connor's observation, applicable to the description of Socrates' "possession" by the local Nymphs in the *Phaedrus*, that there is a "close link between the nympholept and a specific location" (p. 162). More importantly, Connor concludes from a wide variety of extant sources that "nympholepsy is not an illness or form of madness, but a state of heightened awareness and expression" (p. 164).

13. Cf. 238d5 for an early example of Socrates' claim that Phaedrus is 'responsible' (αἴτιος) for his poetic outburst. Another reference to Phaedrus' spell over Socrates occurs at 242e1.

himself to be inspired,[15] even if his reference to the dithyrambic style may suggest that his relationship to the Muses is not what he thinks it ought to be. He is inspired at this point by the local Nymphs and not by the Muses.

It must be noted that at this point in the *Phaedrus*, Plato highlights Socrates' premonition that the views expressed in his first speech may lead to something disastrous. Exactly what Socrates fears is left ambiguous. However, he expresses the hope that 'the imminent danger may be avoided' in the course of his subsequent words. He tells Phaedrus to listen to the rest of his excursus with the hope that 'the forthcoming threat' may be avoided: ἀλλὰ τὰ λοιπὰ ἄκουε· ἴσως γὰρ κἂν ἀποτράποιτο τὸ ἐπιόν (238d5-6). Although one may understand τὸ ἐπιόν as designating 'the threatening nympholepsy' of Socrates,[16] it also may be a veiled allusion to the wrath of Eros. Socrates' palinode, itself an apotropaic gesture designed to avert any possible punishment of Socrates for his slighting of Eros, may be foreshadowed here. Since Socrates is portrayed later in the dialogue as being aware of the danger one can incur by casting reproach upon a divinity (the blinding of Stesichorus is an example), it is preferable to view τὸ ἐπιόν as a reference to the possibility of divine retribution inflicted upon mortals. Socrates' use of the verb ἀποτράποιτο here is striking; ἀποτρέπω is usually found in the context of rituals designed to appease the gods and thus 'turn away' or avert their anger.

Socrates' hypothetical speech (λόγος) to the imaginary youth (παῖς) continues at 238d8.[17] One is meant to understand that Phaedrus is the young man to whom Socrates directs his words. He describes the lover as someone who should not be entrusted with the education of the beloved; an older lover

---

14. The dithyramb is mocked in the fifth century by Aristophanes (*Pax* 829). Plato has Hermogenes call the awkward sounding name σελαενονεοάεια, coined by Socrates, διθυραμβῶδες (*Cratylus* 409c3). My interpretation agrees with that of Ferrari 1987.100.

15. Cf. P. Vicaire 1960.199 n.1: "Dans le *Phèdre* l'intention satirique est moins nette: une inspiration authentique va percer dans le discours de Socrate."

16. Cf. De Vries 1969.89 for such an interpretation.

17. Socrates describes the youth at 237b2-3: Ἦν οὕτω δὴ παῖς, μᾶλλον δὲ μειρακίσκος, μάλα καλός· τούτῳ δὲ ἦσαν ἐρασταὶ πάνυ πολλοί.

would make certain that his beloved not come into contact with philosophy, since 'divine philosophy' (ἡ θεία φιλοσοφία), the source of wisdom, threatens the lover's control over the beloved (239b3-c2). Socrates' disparaging depiction of a lover's detrimental influence over the object of his affection is reiterated in the remainder of the speech. His main argument is that contact with a lover is harmful to the education of a young man's soul (241c4-6). The relationship between lover and beloved 'young man' (παῖς) is compared to that between wolf and sheep: ὡς λύκοι ἄρνας ἀγαπῶσιν, ὣς παῖδα φιλοῦσιν ἐρασταί (241d1: 'wolves love sheep just as lovers like young men').[18] It is noteworthy that Socrates ends his speech with a "poetic" proverb that, ironically, can be understood as an αἶνος ('meaningful saying') advising Phaedrus to be wary of old men like Socrates. However, as the dialogue progresses, it becomes clear that Socrates is different from the ἐρασταί ('lovers') he has described here. His attempt to cultivate in Phaedrus an understanding of the central role of philosophy (and, by extension, that of love) as part of the 'education' (παίδευσις) of the human soul makes Socrates himself a counterexample to the type of lover he advises Phaedrus to avoid.

Socrates proclaims that his speech has reached its end. By his use of the colloquial phrase τοῦτ' ἐκεῖνο (241d2), he tells Phaedrus that this is the speech that he would use to counter Lysias'.[19] He states that he will no longer continue his speech to Phaedrus: οὐκέτ' ἂν τὸ πέρα ἀκούσαις ἐμοῦ λέγοντος, ἀλλ' ἤδη σοι τέλος ἐχέτω ὁ λόγος (241d2-3). The emphatic placement of the dative σοι alludes to Socrates' having offered his speech only to please Phaedrus (cf. 236e1-237a6). The young man expresses surprise at Socrates' abrupt ending, especially since Socrates failed to mention the positive attributes of a 'nonlover' (ὁ μὴ ἐρῶν) and the reasons for bestowing favor

---

18. This proverb ends in a hexametric cadence (παῖδα φιλοῦσιν ἐρασταί).

19. Some (e.g. De Vries 1969.102, who accepts the interpretation found in Kühner-Gerth 1955[1].650) understand ἐκεῖνο to refer here to Socrates' own earlier forebodings at 238d1-3. This seems an overly complicated reading; surely one can understand τοῦτ' ἐκεῖνο, ὦ Φαῖδρε simply to mean that Socrates has just completed the type of speech that Phaedrus begged him to recite.

upon a nonlover rather than upon a lover (241d4-7). "Why indeed do you break off now, Socrates?" asks Phaedrus. Socrates' response expresses his own fear at the views he has expressed so far; he does not dare to continue because he fears the power of the inspiration he attributes to the Nymphs. He tells Phaedrus:

> οὐκ ᾔσθου, ὦ μακάριε, ὅτι ἤδη ἔπη φθέγγομαι ἀλλ' οὐκέτι διθυράμβους, καὶ ταῦτα ψέγων; ἐὰν δ' ἐπαινεῖν τὸν ἕτερον ἄρξωμαι, τί με οἴει ποιήσειν; ἆρ' οἶσθ' ὅτι ὑπὸ τῶν Νυμφῶν, αἷς με σὺ προύβαλες ἐκ προνοίας, σαφῶς ἐνθουσιάσω; λέγω οὖν ἑνὶ λόγῳ ὅτι ὅσα τὸν ἕτερον λελοιδορήκαμεν, τῷ ἑτέρῳ τἀναντία τούτων ἀγαθὰ πρόσεστιν. καὶ τί δεῖ μακροῦ λόγου; περὶ γὰρ ἀμφοῖν ἱκανῶς εἴρηται. καὶ οὕτω δὴ ὁ μῦθος ὅτι πάσχειν προσήκει αὐτῷ, τοῦτο πείσεται· κἀγὼ τὸν ποταμὸν τοῦτον διαβὰς ἀπέρχομαι πρὶν ὑπὸ σοῦ τι μεῖζον ἀναγκασθῆναι.
> (241e1-242a2)

> My dear good man, haven't you noticed that I've got beyond dithyramb and am breaking out into verse, despite my faultfinding? What do you suppose I shall do if I start extolling the other type? Don't you see that I shall clearly be possessed by those nymphs into whose clutches you deliberately threw me? I therefore tell you, in one short sentence, that to each evil for which I have abused the one party there is a corresponding good belonging to the other. So why waste words? All has been said that needs saying about them both. And that being so, my story can be left to the fate appropriate to it, and I will take myself off across the river here before you drive me to greater lengths.

This passage echoes Socrates' earlier reference to his imminent possession by the Nymphs (238d1-3); however, he now thinks that by the end of his speech he no longer utters dithyrambs but instead has broken out into epic (241e1: ἤδη ἔπη φθέγγομαι). The shift in Socrates' description of his style from 'almost dithyrambic' (238d2-3: οὐκέτι πόρρω διθυράμβων φθέγγομαι) to 'epic' is important because Socrates is stressing, once he has finished his speech to Phaedrus, how "carried away" he was while talking.[20] He is attempting to disclaim any responsibility for what he has said under the influence of external forces such as the Nymphs; like the poets who, he believes, do not have a true understanding of what they themselves say, Socrates himself has been "possessed." The word he uses to designate his speech, μῦθος (241e8; cf. 237a9), is significant because it implies that Socrates views his speech as a story and not as a Lysianic oration designed to persuade Phaedrus.[21] Socrates sees Phaedrus as the instigator of this μῦθος that deserves to 'suffer' (πάσχειν) a dreadful fate.

That Socrates is anticipating something terrible will happen as a result of his speech is expressed by his apparent attempt to make his way back across the river and leave Phaedrus alone in the supernatural surroundings. However, Phaedrus says that Socrates should stay until the midday heat lessens and, more importantly, he urges Socrates to continue the discussion of the matter at hand.[22] The young man's yearning for more discussion is important in the context of the dialogue because it signifies his readiness to participate in the activity which most typifies a philosopher, a 'lover' of wisdom. In other words, he will be receptive to Socrates' subsequent instruction (παιδεία) on love and philosophy. Although Phaedrus wishes to have more discussion, as the dialogue progresses, Socrates will be the one who does most of the talking.

---

20. Note Socrates' emphasis on oral communication (φθέγγομαι at 238d3 and 241e1). Plato might be setting the stage for Socrates' criticism of the written word later in the dialogue (cf. 275d4 and following). In addition, the fact that Socrates considers his words to be poetic highlights his depiction as someone who is 'possessed'; as Connor 1988.158 n.11 points out, "possessed persons in antiquity were often said to express themselves through verse."

21. Cf. Socrates' reference to a 'myth' (μυθολόγημα), that of Boreas' rape of Oreithuia, at the beginning of the dialogue (229c5). Ferrari 1987.116 comments on Socrates' use of myth in general in the dialogue: "...he cannot espouse myth wholeheartedly, but only as a necessary resource from which he must maintain a careful distance."

22. Plato's presentation of the setting here seems to have erotic overtones. See Nussbaum 1986.472 n.20 for bibliography on the Greek superstition linking summer heat with intense sexual desire.

Although it seems at first that Phaedrus is responsible for stopping Socrates when he starts to cross the river (242a3-6),[23] Socrates makes it clear that something else has prevented him from leaving. He attributes his staying to his 'divine sign' (τὸ δαιμόνιον), which, as in *Apology* 31c-32a, checks him when he is on the verge of doing something (242b8-c1: τὸ δαιμόνιόν τε καὶ τὸ εἰωθὸς σημεῖόν μοι γίγνεσθαι ἐγένετο--ἀεὶ δέ με ἐπίσχει ὃ ἂν μέλλω πράττειν). The prohibitory 'divine sign' seemed to be telling him that he would not be allowed to leave until he 'expiated' (242c3: ἀφοσιώσωμαι) for having committed some wrong against 'the divine' (τὸ θεῖον). His feeling the need to purify himself is significant because, as we shall later see, the palinode represents a form of ancient ritual purification (243a4: καθαρμὸς ἀρχαῖος). In addition, the declaration of his being a 'seer' (μάντις) foreshadows his future description of prophecy as one type of divinely inspired 'madness' (μανία).[24] Although he tries to downplay his prophetic power (242c3-4: εἰμὶ δὴ οὖν μάντις μέν, οὐ πάνυ δὲ σπουδαῖος—'I am a seer, although not a very good one'), he claims to understand the nature of his 'offense' (242c6 and 242d2: ἁμάρτημα).[25] He compares himself to the poet Ibycus, who had expressed the fear that he had somehow offended the gods while gaining renown from mortals. Like Ibycus, Socrates feels fear and perhaps shame at the prospect of offending the gods:

ἐμὲ γὰρ ἔθραξε μέν τι καὶ πάλαι λέγοντα τὸν λόγον, καί
πως ἐδυσωπούμην κατ' Ἴβυκον, μή τι παρὰ θεοῖς
ἀμβλακὼν τιμὰν πρὸς ἀνθρώπων ἀμείψω·

---

23. In his response to Phaedrus' request, Socrates manages to make Phaedrus' enthusiasm for discourse responsible for necessitating his own forthcoming speech (242b4-5).

24. Cf. 244a6-c5 (note especially his etymological word play with μανική and μαντική). See Dodds 1951.64-75 for a discussion of "prophetic madness."

25. Whether or not Socrates' divinatory powers are a basis for his claims to certain knowledge has been the subject of intense scholarly debate. Vlastos 1991 and Brickhouse and Smith 1994 provide opposing viewpoints on precisely this problem.

νῦν δ' ᾔσθημαι τὸ ἁμάρτημα.²⁶

(242c7-d2)

For I felt disturbed some while ago as I was delivering that speech, and had a misgiving lest I might, in the words of Ibycus, "By sinning in the sight of God win high renown from man." But now I realize my sin.

The verb by which he describes his apprehension, ἐδυσωπούμην, conveys Socrates' shamefacedness and alludes to his actual and figurative lack of vision during his first speech to Phaedrus.²⁷ By comparing himself to Ibycus, Socrates already places himself in the ranks of the lyric poets and therefore sets the stage for his forthcoming comparison to Stesichorus.

When Phaedrus asks Socrates what error has been committed, the latter responds that each has provided a terrible speech (242d4-5: δεινόν, ὦ Φαῖδρε, δεινὸν λόγον αὐτός τε ἐκόμισας ἐμέ τε ἠνάγκασας εἰπεῖν).²⁸ Although λόγον is an accusative singular, it refers to the two speeches hitherto offered: the speech of Lysias (as delivered by Phaedrus) and that of Socrates in compliance with Phaedrus' behest. It is important that Socrates regards the two separate speeches as a single speech that is 'foolish and somewhat impious' (242d7: εὐήθη καὶ ὑπό τι ἀσεβῆ). Socrates is again blaming Phaedrus for the views he has been forced to expound; namely, Lysias' views. Socrates' criticism of the speeches presented so far becomes

---

26. See *PMG* 310 for additional references to this fragment of Ibycus. Socrates' introduction to the quotation (242c9: μή τι παρὰ θεοῖς) paraphrases Ibycus' words as quoted by Plutarch *Qu. Conv.* 9.15.2: δέδοικα μή τι πὰρ θεοῖς / ἀμβλακὼν....

27. Cf. note 10 above.

28. See De Vries 1969.107 for a discussion of Plato's "pathetic effect" of anaphora here (δεινόν...δεινόν) and elsewhere in his dialogues. Charles Segal has called my attention to the "richly ambiguous" meaning of δεινός here, especially in light of Socrates' subsequent "palinode" in his second speech. Although Hackforth 1952.51 translates λόγον as 'theory' at 242d4, I agree with De Vries 1969.107 that it means 'speech', since the context makes it clear that Socrates is referring to both Lysias' speech (delivered by Phaedrus) and his own speech which he had been compelled (ἠνάγκασας) by Phaedrus to provide.

explicit in the passage beginning at 242d11. He claims that Phaedrus, having placed a spell on his (i.e., Socrates') mouth, bewitched him into presenting Phaedrus' own impious λόγος regarding love; in other words, Phaedrus has used Socrates as a medium.[29] Later in the dialogue (244a1-2), Socrates explicitly claims that his speech was actually that of Phaedrus. The pair of speeches[30] have treated Eros, which Phaedrus agrees is a god or some type of divine entity, as evil (242e2-4). According to Socrates, the speeches 'do not say anything which is healthy' (τὸ μηδὲν ὑγιὲς λέγοντε); they appeal only to 'homunculi' (243a: ἀνθρωπίσκους). Consequently, since his mouth was 'drugged' by Phaedrus into speaking 'unhealthy' words, Socrates feels the need to purify himself (243a2-3: ἐμοὶ μὲν οὖν, ὦ φίλε, καθήρασθαι ἀνάγκη).[31]

The act of ritualized purification takes the form of Socrates' subsequent recantation with the palinode of Stesichorus serving as its exemplar. He mentions an 'ancient rite of purification' (καθαρμὸς ἀρχαῖος) available to 'those who err with regard to the telling of myths':

ἔστιν δὲ τοῖς ἁμαρτάνουσι περὶ μυθολογίαν καθαρμὸς ἀρχαῖος, ὃν Ὅμηρος μὲν οὐκ ᾔσθετο, Στησίχορος δέ. τῶν γὰρ ὀμμάτων στερηθεὶς διὰ τὴν Ἑλένης κακηγορίαν οὐκ ἠγνόησεν

---

29. Socrates' description of his being Phaedrus' mouthpiece is indeed graphic; he characterizes Phaedrus' λόγος ('speech') with the following relative clause (242d11-e1): ὃς διὰ ἐμοῦ τοῦ στόματος καταφαρμακευθέντος ὑπὸ σοῦ ἐλέχθη.

30. The dual nominative τὼ λόγω (242e3) refers to the speeches presented by the two interlocutors. It is interesting to note that both Phaedrus and Socrates offer speeches which, in some sense, are not their own. Phaedrus delivers Lysias' speech while Socrates himself now maintains that he delivered Phaedrus' speech. Perhaps Socrates is suggesting that Lysias bewitched Phaedrus who, in turn, bewitched Socrates.

31. Socrates' diction throughout the *Phaedrus* is permeated by his metaphorical use of "pharmaceutical" and "purificatory" terminology (for example, 242e1: καταφαρμακευθέντος; cf. 229c8: Φαρμακεία, mentioned in Socrates' reference to the 'myth' [229c5: μυθολόγημα] dealing with the rape of Oreithuia by Boreas; in addition to 243a3 and a4 [καθήρασθαι, καθαρμός], cf. 243d5: ἀποκλύσασθαι ['to wash away']). See Derrida 1972.69-198 for his discussion of "la pharmacie de Platon."

ὥσπερ "Ομηρος, ἀλλ' ἅτε μουσικὸς ὢν ἔγνω τὴν αἰτίαν, καὶποιεῖ εὐθὺς—
οὐκ ἔστ' ἔτυμος λόγος οὗτος,
οὐδ' ἔβας ἐν νηυσὶν εὐσέλμοις,
οὐδ' ἵκεο Πέργαμα Τροίας·
καὶ ποιήσας δὴ πᾶσαν τὴν καλουμένην Παλινῳδίαν παραχρῆμα ἀνέβλεψεν.

(243a3-b3)

Now for such as offend in speaking of gods and heroes there is an ancient mode of purification, which was known to Stesichorus, though not to Homer. When Stesichorus lost the sight of his eyes because of his defamation of Helen, he was not, like Homer, at a loss to know why. As a true artist he understood the reason, and promptly wrote the lines:
    False, false the tale.
    Thou never didst sail in the well-decked ships
    Nor come to the towers of Troy.
And after finishing the composition of his so-called palinode he straightway recovered his sight.

Although the possible form (or 'forms') of Stesichorus' use of the "palinode" as a vehicle for retraction has been the subject of much scholarly debate, especially since the discovery of *P.Oxy.* 2506 (fr. 26, col. 1), Plato's reference to it in the above passage has not been studied with regard to its role within the context of the dialogue itself.[32] The description of the palinode as a καθαρμὸς ἀρχαῖος is in itself significant because Plato has Socrates portray the poetic practices of Stesichorus and, by analogy, those of Socrates, in quasi-ritualistic terms.[33] In order to avert the wrath of a deity, religious practice necessitates the performance of an apotropaic ritual. Socrates' reference to Stesi-

---

32. The controversy surrounding Stesichorus' palinode stems from the supposed incompatibility between references to a single palinode, found in the *Phaedrus* and in Isocrates' *Helen* 10.64, and those describing two separate palinodes (e.g., *P.Oxy.* 2506, fr. 26, col. 1 = *PMGF* I 193 Davies). See Cingano 1982.17-33 for a study of some neglected testimonia which suggest that Stesichorus composed two palinodes.
33. Cf. Sider 1989.426 n.12 for bibliography on "verbal καθαρμός."

chorus fuses the realm of poetry, the medium for μυθολογία ('the telling of myths'), with that of ritual purification.

Stesichorus' palinode then is not just a work of poetry; it is an act of religious significance. Such a depiction of Stesichorus' palinode is important for the dialogue as a whole because Socrates' own palinode is intended not only to protect Socrates from the possible retribution of Eros but also to initiate the young Phaedrus into philosophy. Socrates subsequently attributes to philosophy the religious power he earlier ascribes to poetry (exemplified by Stesichorus' palinode). Consequently, he concludes that the soul of the philosopher alone is made perfect by complete initiation into the mysteries (249c7-8: τελέους ἀεὶ τελετὰς τελούμενος, τέλεος ὄντως μόνος γίγνεται).[34] Instead of Stesichorus, the poet described as μουσικός (243a6), Socrates the philosopher becomes the performer of "correct" ritual within the context of his dialogue with Phaedrus. Stesichorus' phrase οὐκ ἔστ' ἔτυμος λόγος οὗτος is not simply a retraction of views which are somehow misguided. Since Socrates appropriates the phrase for himself when he begins his own palinode at 244a3, he imparts to these words a ritual significance. This quotation from Stesichorus may be said to provide a "catch-phrase" for the rite of recantation in the palinode of Socrates.

Socrates' ritual of recantation resembles that of Stesichorus not only by its adoption of the poet's own *persona*[35] and words (at the beginning of the palinode to Eros) but also by its reference to the restoration of the sight of those guilty of 'slander' (cf. 243a6 and 243b5: κακηγορία). Socrates says that Stesichorus 'immediately regained his sight after having

---

34. Note that one finds the terms καθαρμός and τελετή mentioned together at 244e2 (the description of the "second" type of madness which, by prophesying 'rites of purification and initiation', finds deliverance from afflictions brought about by the former transgressions of one's ancestors).

35. Socrates prefaces his palinode with the comment that the first speech (i.e., the speech he delivered against Eros) was that of Phaedrus, whereas the second speech which he is about to deliver is that of Stesichorus of Himera, the son of Euphemus (243e9-244a3: οὑτωσὶ τοίνυν, ὦ παῖ καλέ, ἐννόησον, ὡς ὁ μὲν πρότερος ἦν λόγος Φαίδρου τοῦ Πυθοκλέους, Μυρρινουσίου ἀνδρός· ὃν δὲ μέλλω λέγειν, Στησιχόρου τοῦ Εὐφήμου, Ἱμεραίου).

completed his palinode' (243b2-3).[36] In other words, Stesichorus' sudden blindness prompted his composing the palinode to appease Helen. Socrates, however, boasts that he is wiser than Homer and Stesichorus and, consequently, he will offer his palinode before becoming the victim of possible divine retribution:

ἐγὼ οὖν σοφώτερος ἐκείνων γενήσομαι κατ' αὐτό γε
τοῦτο· πρὶν γάρ τι παθεῖν διὰ τὴν τοῦ Ἔρωτος
κακηγορίαν πειράσομαι αὐτῷ ἀποδοῦναι τὴν παλινῳδίαν,
γυμνῇ τῇ κεφαλῇ καὶ οὐχ ὥσπερ τότε ὑπ' αἰσχύνης
ἐγκεκαλυμμένος.
(243b3-7)

Now it's here that I shall show greater wisdom than these poets. I shall attempt to make my due palinode to Love before any harm comes to me for my defamation of him, and no longer veiling my head for shame, but uncovered.

Socrates' unveiling his head at this moment is significant. Like Stesichorus, he performs a gesture; however, Socrates regains his sight before delivering his palinode to Eros, while Stesichorus must complete his palinode to Helen before he can see again. The palinode, which is an act of atonement in the case of Stesichorus, becomes an apotropaic gesture for Socrates. As a result, the latter can be said to surpass the former. Stesichorus, whose own style may be considered "Homeric," transcends

---

36. I translate in accordance with the interpretation offered by Sider 1989.426-430. He argues that Stesichorus' blinding "is essentially to be understood as an act of theater in which Stesichorus, either alone or, more likely, in company with a body of singer-dancers, himself danced and sung as if unable to see" (p. 430). Sider, combining the references to Stesichorus' palinode in the *Phaedrus* and in Isocrates' *Helen*, hypothesizes that Stesichorus acted out his having been struck blind by Helen; he 'stood up' (Isocrates' *Helen* 10.64: ἀνέστη) in the midst of his song, acted out his blindness which, he realized, was caused by having blasphemed in some way against Helen soon after he had begun to sing, recanted in the 'so-called palinode' and thereafter immediately regained his vision.

Homer and is therefore called μουσικός by Socrates (243a6).[37] In a similar vein, Socrates' first speech resembles that of Lysias but now the message of his second speech (the palinode to Eros) will be superior to that of Lysias. Perhaps it can be said that the composer of a palinode not only recants but also surpasses his predecessor's work on a given theme.

Although the explicit goal of Socrates' own palinode is to rescind the views expressed in his former speech which in essence agreed with that of Lysias, an implicit connection between Socrates and another orator, namely, Isocrates, is achieved by Plato's having Socrates quote Stesichorus' palinode. Isocrates also refers to Stesichorus' palinode when describing Helen's 'power' (δύναμις) in his famous encomium:

> ἐνεδείξατο δὲ καὶ Στησιχόρῳ τῷ ποιητῇ τὴν ἑαυτῆς δύναμιν· ὅτε γὰρ ἀρχόμενος τῆς ᾠδῆς ἐβλασφήμησέ τι περὶ αὐτῆς ἀνέστη τῶν ὀφθαλμῶν ἐστερημένος, ἐπειδὴ δὲ γνοὺς τὴν αἰτίαν τῆς συμφορᾶς τὴν καλουμένην παλινῳδίαν ἐποίησε, πάλιν αὐτὸν εἰς τὴν αὐτὴν φύσιν κατέστησεν.
>
> (*Helen* 10.64)

> And she demonstrated her own power to the poet Stesichorus also; for when he disparaged her in some way at the beginning of his song, he stood up and was deprived of his sight. When he understood the cause of his misfortune, he composed the so-called 'palinode' and she restored him to his original state.

If one compares this passage to Socrates' words at 243a5-b2, a verbal resemblance between the two texts is immediately apparent. Especially striking is the phrase τὴν καλουμένην παλινῳδίαν ('the so-called palinode') found in the two accounts of Stesichorus' blinding. While Isocrates mentions the palinode in the context of his praise of Helen's influence over poets such as

---

37. Perhaps one can claim that just as Stesichorus "outdoes" Homer, Socrates, who views his first speech as dithyrambic and epic, sees himself as surpassing the lyric poet Stesichorus, the epic poet Homer and, of course, the 'maker' (ποιητής; cf. 234e6) of speeches, Lysias.

Stesichorus and Homer, Socrates refers to the palinode as an example of Stesichorus' superiority over Homer with respect to μουσική. Like Robert Howland, Christoph Eucken sees Socrates' reference to Stesichorus' palinode in the *Phaedrus* as part of Plato's overall attack on the oratory of Isocrates.[38] Eucken writes: "Wie Platon Stesichoros gegen Homer so stellt er sich selbst gegen Isokrates."[39] Unlike Socrates, Isocrates confirms the portrayal of Helen by the epic poets, since he later claims that some of the Homeridae regard Helen as having 'commanded' (προσέταξε) Homer to compose the *Iliad* and credit her for the poem's beauty and renown (10.65). Thus, Eucken sees a dichotomy between the following pairs: Homer/Isocrates and Stesichorus/Plato (Socrates).

Such an interpretation, although oversimplified, is attractive because Isocrates is mentioned by name at the end of the dialogue. Phaedrus asks what message Socrates imparts to 'the fair Isocrates' (278e8: Ἰσοκράτη τὸν καλόν); Socrates responds with a backhanded compliment referring to Isocrates' literary superiority over Lysias and his innate predisposition toward φιλοσοφία (279a3-b1).[40] Isocrates then can be considered as part of Plato's intended audience in the *Phaedrus*. Although the relationship between the references to Stesichorus' palinode by Isocrates and Plato is uncertain, one can confidently assert that Socrates is portrayed in the dialogue as the enemy of oratory and the advocate of philosophy, which, as practiced by Socrates upon the young Phaedrus, replaces the stories of Homer and Stesichorus with its own brand of μυθολογία.

Before concluding this brief study of the role of lyric poetry in the dialogue, I would like to focus upon certain other aspects of Socrates' final speech which are worthy of mention. Socrates begins his "palinode" with the assertion that a lover 'is mad' (244a5: μαίνεται), and he compares this type of madness to

---

38. Cf. R. L. Howland 1937.154 and Eucken 1983.115-120.
39. Eucken 1983.116.
40. See De Vries 1969.264 for the ambiguity of the word φιλοσοφία in this context. Is Socrates ironically referring to Isocrates' notion of 'philosophy'? Perhaps one is meant to conclude that, just as Isocrates can picture himself as a philosopher, Socrates can depict himself as a poet like Stesichorus.

divinely inspired prophecy.[41] Plato later depicts Socrates as a type of seer who has a special knowledge of what is beyond the heavens. Socrates is superior to any poet, present or future, because he alone can see 'the region' (τὸν τόπον) where true 'being' (οὐσία) resides (247c3-d1). Plato has Socrates present himself as the only poet who 'will sing worthily' (247c4: ὑμνήσει κατ' ἀξίαν) on this subject. Socrates' words at the beginning of his account of this region (ἔχει δὲ ὧδε) are those of an inspired poet beginning his 'song' (ὕμνος).

The theme of the inspiration of Socrates by external forces is stressed throughout the *Phaedrus*. At one point, he claims that, 'because of his inspired state' (263d1-2: διὰ τὸν ἐνθουσιαστικόν), he cannot remember whether or not he defined ἔρως at the beginning of his last speech. As has been mentioned earlier, he attributes his inspiration to a variety of sources. Along with the Muses, the Nymphs, and other local deities (e.g. Pan at 263d6), the cicadas as 'prophets' of the Muses and 'singers' (ᾠδοί) inspire Socrates with oratorical skill (262d3-6). More importantly, we are told by Socrates in an elaborate myth supposedly known by anyone who is 'a lover of the Muses' (259b5: φιλόμουσον ἄνδρα) that the cicadas help mankind win the favor of the Muses (259b5-d7). The cicadas were once men who predated the Muses. When the Muses provided them with the gift of song, they found such pleasure in singing that they forgot to eat and drink and subsequently died. It is from these men that the race of cicadas was born. The Muses make it possible for the cicadas to sing constantly without having any need for sustenance. Upon their death, the cicadas report to the Muses concerning the honor which individual mortals pay to them individually (259c6: τίς τίνα αὐτῶν τιμᾷ τῶν ἐνθάδε). Socrates says that Kalliope and Ourania are the Muses who have a reciprocal relationship with philosophers; philosophers honor the μουσική of this pair which is concerned with heaven and with the stories of gods and men (259d5-7). Surely Socrates regards himself as a devotee of this type of μουσική.

The relationship between mortals and the Muses seems to be one of symbiosis. Perhaps the prayer to Pan and the other local deities at the end of the *Phaedrus* can be understood as Socrates'

---

41. See note 24 above.

own display of honoring the external sources of his inspiration while obtaining their favor:

> ὦ φίλε Πᾶν τε καὶ ἄλλοι ὅσοι τῇδε θεοί, δοίητέ μοι καλῷ γενέσθαι τἄνδοθεν· ἔξωθεν δὲ ὅσα ἔχω, τοῖς ἐντὸς εἶναί μοι φίλια. πλούσιον δὲ νομίζοιμι τὸν σοφόν· τὸ δὲ χρυσοῦ πλῆθος εἴη μοι ὅσον μήτε φέρειν μήτε ἄγειν δύναιτο ἄλλος ἢ ὁ σώφρων.
> (279b8-c3)

> Dear Pan, and all ye other gods that dwell in this place, grant that I may become fair within, and that such outward things as I have may not war against the spirit within me. May I count him rich who is wise, and as for gold, may I possess so much of it as only a temperate man might bear and carry with him.

There appears to be a relationship between "the external" and "the internal" in the first and second parts of the prayer. Socrates asks 'to become fair within'. Perhaps Socrates' being in the presence of the beauty of Phaedrus, as well as that of the surroundings, will result in Socrates' becoming beautiful in both his body (representing "the external") and his soul (representing "the internal"). One is reminded of Socrates' remarks at 256d-e when he says that the souls of lovers will develop the same plumage. His second request, a prayer for a "friendly" relationship between his external possessions and his internal ones, can be interpreted as an expression of Socrates' acknowledgment of the importance of divine inspiration combined with his fear of its power to beguile the soul. Like the cicada, Socrates can be understood to have no need for material things such as 'gold' (χρυσός) which, like food and drink, are regarded by nonphilosophers as essential for life.[42] The wisdom of the philosopher is the greatest possible wealth. The blessings of Eros thus resemble the blessings Socrates requests from Pan and the local deities.[43] Μουσική has become the heightened

---

42. I understand both ὁ σοφός and ὁ σώφρων as designations for a philosopher.
43. Cf. Clay 1979.348: "In the *Phaedrus*, Eros and Pan are connected."

appreciation of the interrelationship between the various sorts of divinely inspired madness: prophecy, poetic sensibility, and love. In addition, it refers to the best possible relationship one can have with the external source of inspiration, the Muses: a relationship based on φιλοσοφία.[44] Plato ends the dialogue with a Socrates who has been inspired again by his surroundings. His inspiration has enabled him to be a lyric poet, a prophet, and, more importantly with respect to the young Phaedrus, a lover.

---

44. Cf. 259d3-8.

# 5

# CONCLUSION

My goal in this study has been to consider three famous lyric quotations in their respective contexts within the works of Plato. The interpretation of the Simonides poem in the *Protagoras*, I argued in chapter two, is an integral part of the dialogue between Socrates and his interlocutor, the sophist Protagoras. Although Socrates' exegesis has been regarded by many as a lengthy digression which adds nothing to the dialogue as a whole, a careful look at the contents and purpose of his remarks suggests the contrary. Plato has Socrates provide a fundamentally sound interpretation of the meaning of Simonides' words, even though Protagoras is portrayed as having introduced the discussion of the poem's meaning in such a way that it would be difficult to defend the lyric poet Simonides against the sophist's charge of self-contradiction. Socrates' remarks following his own "philo–sophical" approach to the poem are significant. Discussion regarding the interpretation of poetry is deemed unbefitting to educated men (347b8 ff.).

The third chapter focused upon Callicles' quotation of Pindar in the *Gorgias*. A purposeful misquotation of Pindar's words placed in the mouth of Callicles by Plato is not altogether implausible in light of the quotation's context. The reading of the manuscripts, βιαιῶν τὸ δικαιότατον, should not necessarily be emended in favor of the correct Pindaric text, δικαιῶν τὸ βιαιότατον. A misquotation on the part of Callicles not only suits the immediate context of the Pindaric reference but also adds vividness to the characterization of Callicles.

Socrates' quotation of Stesichorus' palinode in the *Phaedrus* was discussed in the fourth chapter. Like Stesichorus, Socrates composes his own palinode in order to avert potential divine retribution. Plato's portrayal of Socrates as μουσικός ('one who has a true relationship with the Muses') is significant in light of Socrates' comments to the young Phaedrus regarding the nature of love and poetry, which are described as divinely inspired types of μανία ('madness'). The description of the poet in the *Ion* might also be applicable to the depiction of Socrates in the *Phaedrus*:

> κοῦφον γὰρ χρῆμα ποιητής ἐστιν καὶ πτηνὸν καὶ ἱερόν, καὶ οὐ πρότερον οἷός τε ποιεῖν πρὶν ἂν ἔνθεός τε γένηται καὶ ἔκφρων καὶ ὁ νοῦς μηκέτι ἐν αὐτῷ ἐνῇ.
> (*Ion* 534b3-6)

For a poet is a light, winged and holy thing, and he is not able to compose until he is inspired and beside himself, and his mind is no longer within him.

Plato portrays Socrates as more than a philosopher; indeed, his poetical sensibility places him in the ranks of the lyric poets whom he quotes.

# BIBLIOGRAPHY

Adrados, F. R. *Orígenes de la lírica griega*. Madrid, 1976.
Barker, A. *Greek Musical Writings* (vol.1). Cambridge, 1984.
Beazley, J. D. "Citharoedus." *Journal of Hellenic Studies* 42 (1922): 70-98.
Benardete, S. *The Rhetoric of Morality and Philosophy: Plato's Gorgias and Phaedrus*. Chicago, 1991.
Bowra, C. M. *Greek Lyric Poetry* (2nd ed.). Oxford, 1961.
_____. "The Two Palinodes of Stesichorus." *Classical Review* 13 (1963): 245 ff.
Brickhouse, T. C., and N. D. Smith. *Plato's Socrates*. Oxford, 1994.
Burger, R. *Plato's Phaedrus: A Defense of a Philosophic Art of Writing*. Alabama, 1980.
Burn, A. R. *The Lyric Age of Greece*. London, 1960.
Burnet, J., ed. *Platonis opera* (vols. 1-5). Oxford, 1900-1907.
Campbell, D. A. *The Golden Lyre: The Themes of the Greek Lyric Poets*. London, 1983.
Carson, A. "How Not to Read a Poem." *Classical Philology* 87 (1992): 110-130.
Cerri, G. "Il passagio dalla cultura orale alla cultura di comunicazione scritta nell'età di Platone." *Quaderni Urbinati di Cultura Classica* 8 (1969): 119-133.
Cingano, E. "Quante testimonianze sulle palinodie di Stesicoro?" *Quaderni Urbinati di Cultura Classica* n.s. 12 (1982): 21-33.
Clay, D. "Socrates' Prayer to Pan." In *Arktouros*, eds. G. Bowersock, et al. Berlin, 1979: 345-353.
Connor, W. R. "Seized by the Nymphs: Nympholepsy and Symbolic Expression in Classical Greece." *Classical Antiquity* 7 (1988): 155-189.

Crotty, K. *Song and Action: The Victory Odes of Pindar.* Baltimore, 1982.
Davies, M. "Derivative and Proverbial Testimonia Concerning Stesichorus' 'Palinode'." *Quaderni Urbinati di Cultura Classica* n.s. 12 (1982): 7-16.
Davison, J. A. *From Archilochus to Pindar: Papers on Greek Literature of the Archaic Period.* London, 1968.
De Martino, F. "Imitando la palinodia (Stesicoro e Platone)." *Giornale italiano di filologia* n.s. 10 (1979): 255-260.
Derrida, J. "La pharmacie de Platon." In *La dissémination.* Paris, 1972: 69-198.
Descat, R. "Idéologie et communication dans la poésie grecque archaïque." *Quaderni Urbinati di Cultura Classica* n.s. 9 (1981): 7-27.
Des Places, É. *Pindare et Platon.* Paris, 1949.
———. "Simonide et Socrate dans le *Protagoras* de Platon." *Les études classiques* 37 (1969): 236-244.
De Vries, G. J. *A Commentary on the Phaedrus of Plato.* Amsterdam, 1969.
Dickie, M. "The Argument and Form of Simonides 542 PMG." *Harvard Studies in Classical Philology* 82 (1978): 21-33.
Diels, H., and W. Kranz, eds. *Die Fragmente der Vorsokratiker,* I-III (11th ed). Berlin, 1964.
Dindorf, W., ed. *Aelius Aristides* (3 vols.). Leipzig, 1829.
Dodds, E. R. *The Greeks and the Irrational.* Berkeley, 1951.
———. *Plato: Gorgias.* Oxford, 1959.
Donlan, W. "Simonides, fr. 4 D and P. Oxy. 2432." *Transactions of the American Philological Association* 100 (1969): 71-95.
Edmonds, J. M., ed. *Lyra Graeca* (3 vols.). London, 1922-27 (Loeb Classical Library).
Eucken, C. *Isokrates: Seine Positionen in der Auseinandersetzung mit den zeitgenössischen Philosophen.* Berlin, 1983.
Fatouros, G. *Index verborum zur frühgriechischen Lyrik.* Heidelberg, 1966.
Ferrari, G. R. F. *Listening to the Cicadas: A Study of Plato's Phaedrus.* Cambridge, 1987.
Foerster, R., ed. *Libanii Opera* (vol. 5). Leipzig, 1909.
Fortenbaugh, W. "Plato *Phaedrus* 235c3." *Classical Philology* 61 (1966): 108-109.

Fränkel, H. *Dichtung und Philosophie des frühen Griechentums* (3rd ed.). Munich, 1969.
Frede, D. "The Impossibility of Perfection: Socrates' Criticism of Simonides' Poem in the *Protagoras*." *Review of Metaphysics* 39 (1986): 729-753.
Friedländer, P. *Plato* (trans. H. Meyerhoff, 3 vols.). Princeton, 1964.
Gaiser, K. "Das Gold der Weisheit: Zum Gebet des Philosophen am Schluß des Phaidros." *Rheinisches Museum* 132 (1989): 105-140.
Gentili, B. *Poetry and Its Public in Ancient Greece* (trans. A. T. Cole). Baltimore, 1988.
———. "Studi su Simonide, II: Simonide e Platone." *Maia* 16 (1964): 278-306.
Gigante, M. *ΝΟΜΟΣ ΒΑΣΙΛΕΥΣ*. Naples, 1956.
———. "Nuovi resti dell'ode Pindarica." In *Atti del XI. Congresso Internazionale di Papirologia*. Milan, 1966: 286-311.
Giuliano, F. M. "Esegesi letteraria in Platone: la discussione sul carme simonideo nel *Protagora*." *Studi Classici e Orientali* 41 (1991): 105-190.
Görgemanns, H. "Zur Deutung der Szene am Ilissos in Platons *Phaidros*." In *Philanthropia kai Eusebeia* (eds. G. Most, et al.). Göttingen, 1993: 122-147.
Goldberg, L. *A Commentary on Plato's Protagoras*. New York, 1983.
Grieser, H. "Nomos: Ein Beitrag zur griechischen Musikgeschichte." Ph.D. diss. Heidelberg, 1937.
Griswold, C. *Self-Knowledge in Plato's Phaedrus*. New Haven, 1986.
Grote, D. "Callicles' Use of Pindar's Νόμος Βασιλεύς: Gorgias 484b." *Classical Journal* 90 (1994): 21-31.
Guthrie, W. K. C. *The Sophists*, vol. 3, part I of *A History of Greek Philosophy*. Cambridge, 1969.
Hackforth, R. *Plato's Phaedrus*. Cambridge, 1952.
Hamilton, E., and H. Cairns, eds. *The Collected Dialogues of Plato*. Princeton, 1961.
Heinimann, F. *Nomos und Physis*. Basel, 1945.
Havelock, E. *The Literate Revolution in Greece and Its Cultural Consequences*. Princeton, 1982.

Howland, R. L. "The Attack on Isocrates in the *Phaedrus*." *Classical Quarterly* 31 (1937): 151-159.
Huchzermeyer, H. *Aulos und Kithara in der griechischen Musik bis zum Ausgang der klassischen Zeit.* Emsdetten, 1931.
Irigoin, J. *Histoire du texte de Pindare.* Paris, 1952.
Kerford, G. B. *The Sophistic Movement.* Cambridge, 1981.
Kirkwood, G. M. *Early Greek Monody.* Ithaca, 1974.
Koller, H. *Musik und Dichtung im alten Griechenland.* Bern and Munich, 1963.
Kühner, R., and B. Gerth. *Ausführliche Grammatik der griechischen Sprache* I. Leverkusen, 1955.
Labarbe, J. *L'Homère de Platon.* Liège, 1949.
Lanata, G., ed. *Poetica pre-Platonica.* Florence, 1963.
Lewis, J. M. "Eros and the *Polis* in Theognis Book II." In *Theognis of Megara: Poetry and the Polis* (eds. T. J. Figueira and G. Nagy). Baltimore, 1985: 197-222.
Lippman, E. *Musical Thought in Ancient Greece.* New York and London, 1964.
Lloyd-Jones, H. "Pindar Fr. 169" *Harvard Studies in Classical Philology* 76 (1972): 45-56 (=154-165 in *Greek Epic, Lyric and Tragedy.* Oxford, 1990).
Lobel, E., ed. *The Oxyrhynchus Papyri, Part XXVI.* London, 1961.
Lobel, E., and D. Page, eds. *Poetarum Lesbiorum Fragmenta.* Oxford, 1955.
Maas, M., and J. Snyder. *Stringed Instruments of Greece.* New Haven, 1989.
Maehler, H. *Die Auffassung des Dichterberufs im frühen Griechentum bis zur Zeit Pindars.* Göttingen, 1963.
Markowski, H. *De Libanio Socratis defensore* (Breslauer Philologische Abhandlungen 40). Breslau, 1910.
Massenzio, M. "Il poeta che vola: Conoscenza estatica, comunicazione orale e linguaggio dei sentimenti nello *Ione* di Platone." In *Oralità: Cultura, letteratura, discorso* (eds. B. Gentili and G. Paioni). Rome, 1985: 161-174.
Moravcsik, J., and P. Temko, eds. *Plato on Beauty, Wisdom, and the Arts.* Totowa, New Jersey, 1982.
Most, G. "The Challenge of the Context. Simonides' Scopas in Plato's *Protagoras*." summarized in *American Philological Association Abstracts* for 1988 (1989): 103.

Motte, A. "L'aventure spirituelle du *Phèdre* et la prière." In *Understanding the Phaedrus* (ed. L. Rossetti). Sankt Augustin, 1992: 320-323.
Moutsopoulos, E. *La musique dans l'œuvre de Platon.* Paris, 1959.
Murray, P. "Poetic Inspiration in Early Greece." *Journal of Hellenic Studies* 101 (1981): 87-100.
Nagy, G. *The Best of the Achaeans.* Baltimore, 1979.
_____. "Early Greek Views of Poets and Poetry." In *Cambridge History of Literary Criticism* I (ed. G. Kennedy). Cambridge, 1989: 1-77.
_____. *Pindar's Homer.* Baltimore, 1990.
Nauck, A., ed. *Tragicorum Graecorum Fragmenta* (2nd ed.). Leipzig, 1889.
Nicosia, S. *Tradizione testuale diretta e indiretta dei poeti di Lesbo.* Rome, 1976.
Nietzsche, F. *Zur Genealogie der Moral.* Leipzig, 1887.
Nightingale, Andrea. *Genres in Dialogue: Plato and the Construct of Philosophy.* Cambridge, 1996.
Nussbaum, M. *The Fragility of Goodness.* Cambridge, 1986.
Ostwald, M. "Pindar, Nomos and Heracles." *Harvard Studies in Classical Philology* 69 (1965): 109-138.
Pack, R. "Two Sophists and Two Emperors." *Classical Philology* 42 (1947): 17-20.
Page, D., ed. *Poetae Melici Graeci.* Oxford, 1962.
Parry, H. "An Interpretation of Simonides 4 (Diehl)." *Transactions of the American Philological Assocation* 96 (1965): 297- 320.
Pavese, C. "The New Heracles Poem of Pindar." *Harvard Studies in Classical Philology* 72 (1968): 47-88.
Rodis-Lewis, G. "Platon, les muses et le beau." *Bulletin de l'Association Guillaume Budé* (1983): 265-276.
Roebuck, C., ed. *The Muses at Work: Arts, Crafts, and Professions in Ancient Greece and Rome.* Cambridge, Mass., 1969.
Rosenmeyer, T. G. "Plato's Prayer to Pan: *Phaedrus* 279b8-c3." *Hermes* 90 (1962): 34-44.
Rossetti, L., ed. *Understanding the Phaedrus: Proceedings of the II. Symposium Platonicum.* Sankt Augustin, 1992.
Russell, D. A. *Criticism in Antiquity.* Berkeley, 1981.

Schefold, K. *Die Bildnisse der antiken Dichter, Redner, und Denker*. Basel, 1943.
Scodel, R. "Literary Interpretation in Plato's *Protagoras*." *Ancient Philosophy* 6 (1986): 25-37.
Sider, D. "The Blinding of Stesichorus." *Hermes* 117 (1989): 423-431.
Sikes, E. E. *The Greek View of Poetry*. London, 1931.
Sisti, F. "Le due Palinodie di Stesicoro." *Studi Urbinati* n.s. 39 (1965): 301-313.
Snell, B. *Die Entdeckung des Geistes* (4th ed.). Göttingen, 1975.
Snell, B., and H. Maehler, eds. *Pindari Carmina cum Fragmentis* (2 vols.). Leipzig, 1984 (vol. 1, 7th ed.) and 1989 (vol. 2, 1st ed.).
Svenbro, J. "La parole et le marbre: Aux origines de la poétique grecque." Ph. D. diss. Lund, 1976.
Tarrant, D. "Plato's Use of Quotations and Other Illustrative Material." *Classical Quarterly* 45 (1951): 59-67.
Taylor, A. E. *Plato, the Man and his Work*. London, 1960 (reprint of 1926 ed.).
Taylor, C. C. W., trans. *Plato: Protagoras*. Oxford, 1991 (revised ed.).
Theiler, W. "Νόμος ὁ πάντων βασιλεύς." *Museum Helveticum* 22 (1965): 69-80.
Verdam, H. D. "De carmine Simonideo quod interpretatur Plato in Protagora dialogo." *Mnemosyne* 56 (1928): 299-310.
Vicaire, P. *Platon: critique littéraire*. Paris, 1960.
Vlastos, G. *Socrates: Ironist and Moral Philosopher*. Cambridge and Cornell, 1991.
Walsh, G. B. *The Varieties of Enchantment: Early Greek Views of the Nature and Function of Poetry*. Chapel Hill, 1984.
Webster, T. B. L. "Greek Theories of Art and Literature down to 400 B.C." *Classical Quarterly* 33 (1939): 166-179.
Wegner, M. *Das Musikleben der Griechen*. Berlin, 1949.
Wilamowitz-Moellendorff, U. von. *Pindaros*. Berlin, 1922.
_____. *Platon* (2 vols.). Berlin, 1920.
_____. *Sappho und Simonides*. Berlin, 1913.
_____. *Die Textgeschichte der griechischen Lyriker*. Berlin, 1900.

Winnington-Ingram, R. P. *Mode in Ancient Greek Music.* Cambridge, 1936.
Woodbury, L. "Helen and the Palinode." *Phoenix* 21 (1967): 157-176.

# INDEX

Aelius Aristides, 40n2, 46n22, 50-54, 61, 63n75, 64
Aeschylus, 2, 5-7
ἀλήθεια. See truth
Anacreon, 68
Anaxagoras, 4
Antiphon, 42n7
Anytus, 61-63
Archilochus, 3
ἀρετή. See virtue
ᾆσμα. See song
Aristophanes, 4-7; *Clouds*, 5-6; *Frogs*, 2, 5-6; *Peace*, 72n14
Aristotle, *Nic. Ethics*, 22n16; *Poetics*, 13n4; *Rhetoric*, 22n16
Athens, 56n56

βία. See force
blame poetry, 3-4, 27, 52

Callias, 25n36
Callicles, 7, 9, 39-64
catharsis, 78-80
cithara, 6

deontology, 3
dithyramb, 52-53, 71-72
δίκη. See justice

education, 4-8, 6n12, 12, 14, 19-20, 67, 72-74
ἔλεγχος. See refutation

epic poetry, 66, 74
epinician poetry, 32
Eros, 69, 72, 74, 80-82, 84
Euthydemus, 14n6
Euripides, 5-7
exegesis, 4, 9, 31, 33

flute, 35-36
force, 59-64

Gorgias, 4, 7, 9, 39-64

Heraclitus, 49n32
Herakles, 39, 47-54, 57
Herodotus, 47-48
Hesiod, 2-4, 8, 15, 25n25; *Theogony*, 2; *Works and Days*, 14, 15n7
Hippias, 33, 37, 49
Homer, 1, 3-4, 8, 49, 66, 74, 79, 81-83; *Iliad*, 83; *Odyssey*, 2n6

Ibycus, 76-77
inspiration, 2-3
Isocrates, 82-84

justice, 16, 31, 34, 40-41, 44, 46, 49-51, 57-58, 62

καθαρμός. See catharsis, purification
Libanius, 40, 59-64

literary criticism, 1, 5, 16, 23, 39
*logos* (speech, reason), 20, 23, 33, 67, 70, 73, 77-80
long-windedness, 20

love, 26, 28, 30, 49, 55, 65-71, 73-78, 84, 86
lyric poetry, 1, 9, 11, 39, 51, 65-66, 68, 86
Lysias, 66-68, 70, 77, 82

μακρολογία. *See long-windedness*
mania (madness), 68-69, 71, 76, 86
Muses, 2-3, 66-67, 69, 72, 84-86
music, 6-7, 6n12, 8n19, 35-36
μουσική. *See music, poetical sensibility, education*
myth, 4, 74, 78, 80-84
μυθολογία. *See mythology*
mythology, 80-84

Nietzsche, 44, 45nn16-17
*nomos* (custom, law), 41-46, 49, 54-56
nympholepsy, 72-72, 84

ontology, 20
oratory, 67, 82-84

παιδεία. *See education*
palinode, 7, 9, 65-69, 72, 79-83
Pan, 84-85
Phaedrus, 7, 9, 65-86
philosophy, 4, 7, 20, 40n3, 66, 73-75, 80, 82-83, 86
*physis* (nature), 41-45, 49
Pindar, 2-3, 9, 31n44, 39-64
Pittacus, 13-15, 20-21, 23, 25n26, 30, 32, 32n47
Plato, 1-9, 39-40, 49, 52, 58-64, 65-70, 72, 79, 82-86;
*Apology*, 36, 76; *Cratylus*, 4n12, 72n14; *Gorgias*, 4, 7, 9, 39-64; *Laws*, 1, 6n14, 8nn19-20, 9, 50, 60n70; *Phaedrus*, 7, 9, 65-86; *Protagoras*, 4, 4n12, 7, 9, 11-38, 39, 48, 58, 67; *Republic*, 1, 7-9; *Symposium*, 35nn50-51
poet as educator, 2n5, 16-20, 67
poetical sensibility, 14, 66, 84-86
Polycrates, 40, 62-64
praise poetry, 4, 7, 8n20, 9, 27, 52-53, 62, 82
prayer, 84-85
Prodicus, 14-15, 18, 32
prophecy, 68, 76, 84, 86
Protagoras, 11-38, 43n11, 48
purification, 66, 76, 78-80

refutation, 21, 23, 38
rhetoric, 4, 66-67, 69

Sappho, 68
Scopas, 11-12, 20
Semonides, 27
Simonides, 6-7, 9, 11-38, 39, 48
Socrates, 7-9, 11-15, 17-27, 33-38, 39-42, 48, 58, 62-63, 65-86
Solon, 31
song, 19, 82-84
σοφία. *See wisdom*
sophists, 4, 12-18, 20-21, 23, 33, 38, 48-49
Sparta, 20-21
Stesichorus, 7, 9, 65-86
symposia, 6, 34-35

Theagenes of Rhegium, 4
Theognis, 25n25, 31, 35;
Theognidea, 25n28, 64

*Index*

Thucydides, 44n14
truth, 32, 37-38, 41, 44

virtue, 12, 15, 19, 21, 25, 34-35, 38

wisdom, 20-21, 73, 75, 81, 85

Xenophanes, 3-4
Xenophon, 64

# ABOUT THE AUTHOR

Marian Demos received her A.B. in Classics from Princeton University in 1983; she then studied at Corpus Christi College, Oxford. She was awarded her doctorate in Classical Philology from Harvard University in 1991, and is currently an associate professor in the Humanities Program at Florida International University. Her research interests include Greek lyric poetry, Roman Stoicism, and the history of the classical tradition.

www.ingramcontent.com/pod-product-compliance
Lightning Source LLC
Chambersburg PA
CBHW022016300426
44117CB00005B/220